Children in
Time and Space

CHILDREN

Kaoru Yamamoto, Editor

Arizona State University

TEACHERS COLLEGE PRESS

TEACHERS COLLEGE, COLUMBIA UNIVERSITY
NEW YORK AND LONDON   1979

Library of Congress Cataloging in Publication Data

Main entry under title:

Children in time and space.

  Bibliography: p.
  Includes index.
  1. Child development—Addresses, essays, lectures.
I. Yamamoto, Kaoru.
LB1117.C53   301.43'1   79-91

ISBN 0-8077-2553-6

Designed by Romeo Enriquez
Printed in the U.S.A.
1   2   3   4   5   6   7   8
79 80 81 82 83 84 85 86

Original contributions by:

David H. Bauer, *California State University, Chico*
Louise M. Berman, *University of Maryland*
Nathalie J. Gehrke, *Arizona State University*
Beverly Hardcastle Lewis, *Avon (New York) Central School*
Carolyn Emrick Massad, *Educational Testing Service*
Kaoru Yamamoto, *Arizona State University*

With the assistance of:

Jane E. Bergquist, *McLean, Virginia*
Sheila D. Campbell, *University of Alberta, Canada*
O. L. Davis, Jr., *University of Texas at Austin*
L. Lorraine Dibrell, *Texas A & M University*
Henry F. Dizney, *University of Oregon*
Harold D. Drummond, *University of New Mexico*
Marilyn M. Maxson, *Virginia Polytechnic Institute
    and State University*
Gail McEachron-Hirsch, *University of Texas at Austin*
Cynthia L. Walker, *Odom School, Austin (Texas) Independent
    School District*

Contents

Preface

Life is a mystery and a challenge. We all live it in one way or another, but it is no small feat to accept, appreciate, and develop it as a meaningful, organic whole. In their varied yet persistent attempts at making sense, human beings have woven many different patterns of life from a limited number of common threads. Time and space are two of the basic yarns for individual and cultural fabrics of life, and it is these that this volume explores particularly in relation to the world of children.

The book is the third in a series of such interpretive-integrative expositions of the fundamental dimensions of life. Like the two preceding works,* it invites teachers and other helping professionals, both in practice and in preparation, as well as caring parents, to take a new look at familiar human experiences.

Also in common with the two previous projects, this work is the end product of a unique cooperative endeavor among more than a dozen colleagues. When the authors had completed the original versions of their respective chapters to a reasonable degree of satisfaction, they got together with a group of discussants, including

---

*Yamamoto, Kaoru (Ed.). *The Child and his image: Self concept in the early years.* Boston: Houghton Mifflin, 1972; and Yamamoto, Kaoru (Ed.). *Death in the life of children.* West Lafayette, Ind.: Kappa Delta Pi Press, 1978.

parents, classroom teachers and teachers-to-be, teacher educators, curriculum theorists, and educational psychologists, to ponder how their contributions might be improved. As a result of this meeting, the lively flavor of which may be caught in the fourth chapter, each author revised his or her chapter at least once more prior to the final editing of the manuscript.

The critical phase of the face-to-face interaction was supported by the Hogg Foundation for Mental Health, through a grant to Professor O. L. Davis, Jr., of the College of Education, University of Texas at Austin, and myself. The retreat was held in late October 1976 at Rather House of the Episcopal Theological Seminary of the Southwest in Austin, Texas, under the capable coordinating hands of Gail McEachron-Hirsch and George Mehaffey, both doctoral students at the University of Texas at Austin.

All told, then, the book represents the fruit of many people's efforts working together over time and across space. The process is unique and, I believe, so also is the product. Just as each color band of a rainbow reflects the same sunbeam differently, each author discusses the same overall topic in his or her own way. Indeed, part of the strength of this work lies in the diversity of the style and level of discourse, and the wide range will allow individual readers to tune in first to their own wave lengths to receive the shared message. If the reader has not yet given much thought to the whole subject of space and time, he or she may wish to begin with the informal discussion in Chapter 4. One may then return to Chapters 1, 2, and 3 for a systematic view or pursue the more practical concerns examined in Chapters 5, 6, and 7. In any case, I hope that every reader will take full advantage of the collective knowledge, experience, and wisdom of the author team before continuing the study with the help of the suggested sources and materials listed at the end of each chapter.

As the initiator of the project and the editor of this volume, I would like to express my personal appreciation to all who have taken part in this venture directly or indirectly. Thank you!

Kaoru Yamamoto

Children in Time and Space

Space and time are key words in the vocabulary of culture. With them, humans everywhere speak. However, where there is little awareness of the grammar, the message moves people apart. The beginning chapter, written by a specialist in human communication, throws light upon the how and what of the subtle yet persistent voices of time and space.

Time and Space In Space and Time

CAROLYN EMRICK MASSAD

Had we but world enough, and time . . .
Andrew Marvell

The world, it has been said, is four dimensional: three for the space, one for the time. However, the active hands of people change that. People perceive time and space in many different ways, arrange their lives according to their perceptions, apply their interpretations to everyone else's world, and intervene in the here and now. Thus, both *time* and *space* are key words in the vocabulary of culture. Yet how little we have understood these words!

What is time? What is space? For centuries both philosophers and those in the sciences have pondered these questions. Excellent discussions can be found in the literature of anthropology, sociology, psychology, medicine, physics, architecture, philosophy, religion, political science, and other areas of inquiry. The puzzle is not new, and more research is needed, especially research that involves simultaneously several of these disciplines.

1

In the human world, time and space are the framework in which all reality is considered. We cannot think of any real thing except in terms of the conditions of time and space. Cassirer (1944) and Wallis (1968) have said that it is not the mind that conceives time and space; rather it is time and space that fashion and condition the mind. But this is not to say that the forces at work operate in only one direction. For example, the environment in which children develop affects their concepts and views, which, in turn, affect the way growing children perceive the world. Just as people's minds perceive and create their time and space, their creation creates them, the individuals. The existence of cultural differences illustrates this phenomenon well.

The activity that occurs in time and space reflects a "fifth" dimension, the mind. Therefore, if we are concerned about mental development, we must also be concerned about time and space. As Henry (1973) so aptly put it:

> ... space and time are amalgamated with the emotional life of the growing child. Time—cultural time, in the form of changing experiences and changing expectations—presses the personality inexorably on, and together with the press of time the culture offers and imposes changing modes of space. To the inner change there is a corresponding outer change, and while time is experienced as a change in the self and in one's relationships to people, space is experienced as an outer configuration that corresponds to the changes which, as a function of cultural time, are taking place within and toward other people. Our cultural metaphysic must become part of our flesh and bone, part of self, part of our breathing and heartbeat if we want to survive. (p. 119)

To understand an individual necessitates understanding that person's culture. Likewise, to play a role in guiding the development of a child requires an awareness of the child's culture, the child in time and space.

As the work of child psychologists such as Gesell and Piaget indicates, children move through successive stages sequentially and, generally speaking, in a single direction. The rate and distance of the movement, as well as a child's position at any given time, are critical in planning for and guiding future development. Expectations are anchored on an alleged continuum, one that actually consists of many continua. Fortunately the world is beginning to accept the fact that everyone need not be at the same point on each continuum of development. That is to say, for example, a child may be more physically than emotionally mature. Such a situation may give observers the wrong impression—that the child appears to falter, stop, or even backtrack in development. For this reason, specialists in human growth and development encourage parents and educators to view the total child.

Furthermore, in today's shrinking world the child on the way to maturity is expected to move gradually away from his or her home and neighborhood to join in social interactions across wider geographic areas as well as many cultural groups. To be able to fully participate in and gain a deep appreciation of the richness of life, the mature individual must have been exposed to a systematic consideration of time and space and how to handle these fundamental dimensions of culture, not only in terms of his or her own culture but also the culture of others.

TIME CONCEPTS ACROSS TIME

Time is one of the continuing, motivating, and universal experiences of life. It is one of the primary threads that people use in the weave of their experiences. All perceptual, intellectual, and emotional experiences are interwoven with time. The passing of time is a continual *feeling,* but from where does time originate? We continually experience time, yet not by means of the five senses. We cannot taste, see, smell, hear, or touch it. How, then, is time experienced?

People view time from their own particular vantage point. Time is relative to one's cultural values. Therefore, it can be said that the experience of time is conceptual, based on the concept of time held by one's cultural group.

The conception of time as a kind of linear progression measured by the clock and calendar tends to dominate modern Western civilization. We plan our activities for a particular hour, date, and year, moving along in one direction on a continuum. "There is no turning back," we say. In fact, this concept of time so controls our lives that it seems to be an unavoidable necessity of thought.

However, there are other ways of looking at time. People termed primitive by modern civilizations frequently have only very vague ideas about clocks and calendars. Furthermore, most civilizations whose history began prior to our own linear concept of time, which is only two to three hundred years old, have tended to regard time as essentially cyclic in nature. In fact, the very clock and calendar we use to measure a linear progression of time have their origins in this earlier way of viewing time.

Early peoples used the cycle of recurring natural phenomena familiar to them in everyday life as a guide to the passing of time. The most obvious and precise of these phenomena were the alternation of night and day, the phases of the moon, the position of the stars, and the changing of the seasons. Thus, an event that happened "four moons ago" took place when the phase of the moon at the time of the event had recurred four times; a child who had lived through "ten snows" was approximately ten years old. The regularity or predictability of natural events was critical in the concept of time as being cyclic.

Although the concept of time as a linear progression appears to be one of the unique characteristics of the modern Western world, the importance we attach to time itself has cultural precedents in history. The present calendar used for civil purposes throughout the world, the Gregorian calendar named after Pope Gregory XIII who introduced it in 1582, is not the most precise that any civilization has used. For all its sophistication, the Gregorian is not quite as accurate as the Middle American calendars, such as the Mayan calendar devised by astronomer-priests more than a thousand years ago! Other civilizations—the Chinese, Egyptian, Babylonian, Assyrian, Hindu, Hebrew, Greek, Muslim—also developed calendars based on celestial phenomena. Many of these calendars included recurring religious holidays or seasons in which chronology was interwoven with religious concepts; several also were used for astrological purposes, such as determining *favorable* periods for certain activities to take place. Some of these calendars are still in use today along with the Gregorian calendar, the latter being used primarily for government purposes and business transactions.

Calendars other than the Gregorian are used particularly for religious purposes. In fact, it can be said that religious beliefs as well as social and economic conditions have had a powerful influence on peoples' concept of time. For example, the belief in reincarnation by some religious sects appears to adhere to the concept of time as cyclic. On the other hand, the central doctrine of Christianity that the Crucifixion was a unique event in time not subject to repetition implies a linear view of time. Nevertheless, the concept of the Second Coming of Christ seems to indicate a belief in the cyclic nature of time. Even before Christianity, the Hebrews appear to have thought of history as more progressive rather than repetitive, the prophesying of future events holding the promise of the salvation of Israel. However, Alexenburg (1974) has said that the Oriental Jew experiences time as being primarily cyclic. There are celebrations that follow natural cycles that have spatial referents, e.g., the earth's daily motion, the changing phases of the moon, the yearly movements of earth and sun. Also there is the sanctification and celebration of the seventh day as the Sabbath, which is unrelated to any natural cycles that exist in the world of space; instead it belongs to a religious cycle that exists only in the realm of time.

Throughout the medieval period the cyclic and linear concepts of time were in conflict. Those influenced by astronomy and astrology continued to emphasize the cyclic concept. On the other hand, the mercantile class and the rise of a money economy fostered the linear concept of time. The changing attitude toward time in the late Middle Ages and Renaissance was revealed in the visual arts and literature. Artisans could no longer linger over the execution of a work if they were to respond to all the commissions received, a factor that affected their economic security and well-being. Today we have a parallel in the assembly-line production of most goods; time marches on, and we cannot wait for or afford the individual who is very highly specialized in a given craft. Turning to literature, the destructive aspect of time can be seen in Shakespeare's sonnets, which imply that there is no turning back, and in the work of his contemporary, Edmund Spenser, we find the cyclic and linear concepts of time vying with each other.

> But time shall come that all
>   shall changed bee,
> And from thenceforth, none no
>   more change shall see.

On the one hand, Spenser's idea of time was dominated by the figure of the everlasting wheel of change, but, at the same time, his religious convictions led him to conclude that mutability will not last forever. In scientific circles the new concept of linear progress of time was espoused as early as 1602 by Francis Bacon in his *The Masculine Birth of Time*. In addition, several eighteenth century philosophers, such as Leibnitz, Barrow, and Locke, supported the new, forward-looking concept of linear advancement.

Today the puzzle of time is still being explored. The poet, scientist, psychologist, and philosopher attempt to explore the dimensions of our experience of time. The psychologist, along with the biologist, tries to find ways in which time might be experienced. The psychologist, along with the philosopher, attempts to discover the ways in which time experiences mirror our world view.

Although there are many unanswered questions concerning our conscious awareness of time, there is increasing evidence that our bodies contain various biological clocks. Evidence for the existence of internal timing mechanisms in plants and animals has been gathered only relatively recently, in spite of the fact that it has long been known that animals and plants show daily and seasonal rhythms and that certain patterns of behavior occur periodically. The evidence comes mainly from three different areas of research: (1) the study of photoperiodism, the responses of living things to seasonal changes in the length of day and night, such as autumnal coloration and loss of leaves by some plants or the formation of winter pelts in animals; (2) the study of animal navigation, such as the migration of birds or the ability of a lost pet to find its family many miles away; and (3) the study of daily and other periodic rhythms in the behavior and activity of living organisms, such as the opening and closing of flowers and leaves of plants or the sleep requirements of animals.

In people, as in other higher animals, the master clock presumably is located in the central nervous system. Many scientists believe that people function on a 24-hour rhythm. That is, within each 24-hour period, an adult generally requires six to eight hours of sleep, a certain amount of exercise, and so on (Fraser, 1966; Goldberg, 1977). For this reason, air travelers from one continent to another generally experience what is called "jet lag" or physical exhaustion without physical activity. Their biological clocks have been affected by crossing time zones, and thus there are physiological effects.

In addition to the impact of the biological clock, many people are affected by the rhythm of cosmic time. The "Great" time, the all-inclusive and non-passing time of some native Americans, is another quite descriptive term for cosmic time. It is the time that transcends all conceptual time. It is the time by 'which the universe functions, regulating the rhythms of each galaxy. First contemplated by astronomers and religious philosophers, a belief in the power of cosmic time later formed the basis of astrology, which focuses on interpreting the correlation of planetary movements with human experience. Many believe that cosmic time may cause changes in mood and reflections and may even lead to neurotic behavior when its effect on the personality is exceptionally great. For example, Carl G. Jung, one of the great names in the history of the growth of analytical psychology, believed in astrology and had experts in it on his staff.

Indeed, our experience of time has many dimensions. Meerloo (1970) writes of four functions that help people orient themselves to temporal events: the *biological sense of time* (the biological clock), the *estimation of time span,* the *historical sense of time,* and the *sense of continuity.* The biological clock, which has been discussed earlier, is related to the cyclic functions of our organism. These are frequently called *biorhythms,* the annual, seasonal, and diurnal changes one goes through.

The estimation of time span is one's capacity to gauge and measure units of components of our time line, such as days, months, and years. However, since all living things are affected by the rhythms of the universe, if one's rhythmic cadences do not interact favorably with a series of outside stimuli, then an accurate sense of time span is impossible. For example, prisoners in solitary confinement without means of marking the passage of time frequently lose their time sense and experience the sensation of being buried alive.

The historical sense of time, sometimes referred to as the gnostic sense of time, involves the classification of different time elements. The ability to differentiate and distinguish is required, along with memory, so that experiences can be placed along a hypothetical time line.

The sense of continuity is the conscious experience of time becoming part of an occurrence directed at a future goal. It is frequently called the sense of duration because it requires an awareness of the interrelationship of events, implying that an individual has an active part in the filing of historical events. Continuity means taking part in time that does not pass but exists only because the individual has created it through mental filing processes. Naturally, when mental functions are affected, the biological sense of time resists the longest. The other senses of time are more vulnerable since they are more closely tied to human thought processes. Furthermore, it is clear that the senses of time other than the biological sense of time are also more likely to be influenced by and varied due to cultural factors.

Clearly the experiencing of time has affected human history and will undoubtedly have its impact on what is to come. Yet there is much that we do not know about time. Writers, philosophers, psychologists, and scientists are still exploring its multifaceted dimensions.

REFLECTIONS ON PERCEPTION OF SPACE

It is only in recent years that the effects of space on people's behavior has been studied. Yet spatial perceptions have brought about much of history. Expansion and/or colonization by groups of people, events that date back to the beginning of history, were based on the peoples' perceptions of space and their need for more of it. Most wars have been fought over one or more groups' felt need for more territory. At first occupying additional space may have been required because the number of people grew. (We are experiencing something like this today with our concern about overpopulation and the inability to provide for all the people on planet earth.) Later, increasing territorial size came to mean power, much as it does today.

As we ponder the puzzles of time and space, many theories develop. For example, there are those, like the Landsburgs (1974), who propose that people on earth came from other worlds. If this is so, why did people come? Was it overcrowding on the home planet, the effects of a power struggle, or simply inquisitiveness, the desire to know about space other than the one that is occupied? Are we paralleling the activities of these people from outer space in our investigations of the moon and other planets in our solar system?

Interesting as these questions are, knowledge about our immediate environment is of primary importance. Perhaps this realization is what has stimulated the recent study of spatial perception. An individual's shelters, which may be home, office, classroom, corridor, or hospital ward, as well as the surrounding space, affect his or her life and concepts of the world.

As psychologists and anthropologists have lately been discovering, people instinctively mark out zones or territories that they use and react to in many ways. Hall (1969, 1974) has identified four separate distances at which people operate: *intimate, personal, social,* and *public.* Each of these is determined by spatial perceptions. Furthermore, everyone is not equally at ease in handling all four distances. For example, some people feel uncomfortable in public space, such as a stage or lecture platform, while others cannot endure being close to people where their personal or even intimate space is affected. Such discomfort occurs even with those who have a right to expect closeness, such as husbands, wives, and children. Admittedly everyone needs some personal space — a drawer, closet, or room that an individual can call one's own — and may rightfully resent another's uninvited invasion of that personal space. However, many problems in interpersonal relationships can develop when people go to extremes in limiting access to their personal space. When a husband or wife rejects a partner from his or her intimate space, marital problems may quickly develop; when parents prevent children from entering their intimate or personal space, the children may feel insecure, which can lead to other problems.

But how is space perceived? According to Kilpatrick (1961), we never can be aware of the world as such; we are aware only of the impingement of physical forces on the sensory receptors. This statement pinpoints the importance of the sense receptors in constructing the perceptual world that one inhabits. The sensory apparatus of human beings falls into two categories, which Hall (1969) classified as: (1) the distance receptors — the eyes, ears, and nose — which are concerned with examining distant objects, and (2) the immediate receptors — the sense of touch received from skin, muscles, and the like — which are used to examine the world in close proximity. What is critical, however, is the realization that the sense receptors always function in a subjective way. Clearly one's past experience in his or her environment has an impact on how space is perceived. As Bridgman (1954) states, "It is in fact meaningless to try to separate observer and observed, or to speak of an object independent of an observer, or, for that matter, of an observer in the absence of objects of observation" (p. 37).

It is interesting to note that the scientific laws of motion first worked out in detail by Isaac Newton in the 1680s are consistent with Bridgman's statement. That is, an object's speed is relative to a particular observer. Velocities seem to vary from observer to observer. For example, imagine a train passing an observer at 30 miles an hour and a girl on the train throwing a ball at 15 miles an hour in the direction of the train's motion. To the girl throwing the ball and moving with the train, the ball is moving 15 miles an hour. However, to the observer the motions of the train and ball combine, and the ball is moving 45 miles an hour.

Einstein's theory of relativity, so important today in matters concerning energy, grew out of the above theory of relativity because what seemed appropriate for balls thrown from a train does not seem to be applicable for light. Einstein found, for example, that (1) moving objects would have to increase in mass as their speed increased until that mass was infinite at the speed of light and (2) the rate at which time progressed on a moving object would have to decrease as the object's speed increased until time stopped completely when the object was moving at the speed of light. Of course the changes predicted by Einstein are noticeable only when great speed is a factor rather than when ordinary speeds are considered. For typical and simple circumstances, then, Newton's theory of relativity is quite appropriate.

TIME AND SPACE ACROSS SPACE

Thus spoke Chief Seattle of the Dwamish Indians to President Pierce's envoy, Governor Stevenson of the state of Washington, in 1855:

> The Great Chief in Washington sends word that he wishes to buy

our land. How can you buy or sell the sky—the warmth of the land? The idea is strange to us. Yet we do not own the freshness of the air or the sparkle of the water. How can you buy them from us? Every part of this earth is sacred to my people. Every shiny pine needle, every sandy shore, every mist in the dark woods.

The white man does not understand our ways. One portion of the land is the same to him as the next. The earth is not his brother but his enemy, and when he has conquered it, he moves on.

There is no quiet place in the white man's cities. No place to hear the leaves of spring or the rustle of insect wings. What is there to life if a man cannot hear the lovely cry of the whippoorwill or the arguments of the frog around the pond at night?

The whites, too, shall pass—perhaps sooner than other tribes. Continue to contaminate your bed and you will one night suffocate in your own waste. Then the buffalo are all slaughtered, the secret corners of the forest heavy with the scent of many men, and the ripe hills blotted by talking wires. Where is the thicket? Gone. Where is the eagle? Gone. And what is it to say good-bye to the hunt? The end of living. The beginning of survival. (Armstrong, 1971, p. 77)

This message may be more meaningful to us today than it was when it was delivered over a hundred years ago. Not only does it illustrate that different cultures have different perceptions of space or territory, but it also tells us that the voices of time, the descriptions of people's relation to the universe, can extend across time and culture.

Time speaks loudly to make differences in people's life styles. For example, clear contrasts in time perspectives were noted among five neighboring communities in the Southwest inhabited by ex-Texans (white), Hispanic Americans, Navahos, Zunis, and members of the Church of the Latter-day Saints (Kluckhohn and Strodtbeck, 1961). Of the three non-Indian groups, the Mormons were the most strongly oriented to the past, the Hispanic Americans to the present, and the Texans to the future. Their understanding of time, moreover, seems to be of a different order from that of various Indian nations or peoples of other cultures (Priestly, 1968). Misunderstanding and mistrust are often created when people having different conceptualizations of time are in contact with each other.

Cultural differences in space concepts or perceptions are also sources of misunderstanding and mistrust. By way of illustration, the fact that houses in Latin America are frequently built around a patio that is next to the sidewalk but hidden from outsiders by a wall was of concern to some technicians from the United States living in Latin America. These technicians complained of being "left out" of things and wondered what was going on "behind those walls" (Hall, 1959).

No matter how hard a person tries, it is impossible to rid oneself of his or her own culture. One's culture penetrates to the very roots of the nervous system, determining how one perceives the world. The major portion of *culture* lies hidden, beyond voluntary control (Ittleson, 1973; Smith, 1969). Even when our consciousness is raised, when small fragments of culture are elevated to awareness, it is difficult to change. The difficulty lies not only in the fact that one's culture is so personally experienced, but also in the fact that people cannot act or interact in any meaningful way except through the medium of culture.

People and their *extensions* make up one interrelated system reflecting their culture. Peoples' extensions, their speech and actions as well as their artifacts, reflect reality as it exists in their minds. Both consciously and subconsciously people communicate this reality (Massad, 1972). To behave as though people were one thing, and their houses, cities, technologies, religious beliefs, or language were something else, is the greatest mistake that can be made. It is to our advantage to pay more attention to the kinds of extensions we create and to determine how they blend with the extensions of other people. Of course this implies that we must become aware of the culture of other people. If we seek peace and harmony, it is incumbent on us to act; we must make the effort to become aware of our own culture and that of other people. Furthermore, we must have some information about our interrelations with others in order to build a greater awareness and, if necessary, to modify our behavior for improved relations. The ethnic crisis, the urban crisis, and the education crisis are interrelated, all three a result of the interaction that takes place along the cultural dimension, much of which is hidden from view. Can we afford to ignore this cultural dimension? If not, then it behooves us to learn about our own culture and that of others and to learn in such a way that we are aware of the perceptions held and why they are held. We must give ourselves awareness training or raise our consciousness.

TIME SPEAKS

Time frequently speaks more plainly than words. Because it is handled less consciously than language, it conveys less distorted messages than those of the spoken language. Time shouts out where words may lie.

Have you ever experienced long waits for appointments with people who said that what you had come to discuss was of great importance to them? Did you really believe what they said, or did you doubt it because of the lengthy time spent waiting? Or have you ever been awakened at 11:30 p.m. by a phone call from friends who said they were just calling for a little friendly chat? Did you believe what they said, or did you think that perhaps something was wrong and a friend needed help or comfort? People communicate a great deal by time.

Even so, can we be sure of what is being communicated when we deal with people of other cultures? To be certain of the message, one needs to know about the other cultures. For example, Hall (1959, pp. 17-18) tells how a newly appointed attaché to the American embassy in another country forced an appointment with a minister from that country and then became enraged at having to wait 45 minutes in the minister's outer office. What the attaché had not bothered to discover was that he had not waited a suitable period of time before making an appointment—not suitable, that is, according to the customs of his host country. Moreover, a wait of 45 minutes in that country was like a 60 second wait in the United States! It would be absurd for any American to become enraged over a 60 second wait and, to the minister, the attaché was behaving absurdly. Needless to say, his stay in that country was not a happy one.

Advance notice or lead time is quite important in a culture that stresses the importance of schedules, and the rules are learned informally as one grows up. However, rules for lead time in other cultures have seldom been analyzed. Yet consider how important it is to know how much time is needed to prepare people or to have them prepare themselves for what is to come. For example, it is generally unlikely that someone would invite six people for dinner only an hour before the dinner is to begin, unless some preparations had been made previously. At times, and for some, a great deal of advance notice is appropriate, while for others, in some places of the Middle East for example, a period longer than a week would likely be too long.

Further, here in the United States the value of promptness in the context of efficiency is stressed more than anywhere else in the world, except perhaps in places like Japan, Switzerland, and Germany. Many people are obsessed by it. Ulcers and hypertension are claimed to result from the pressures exerted by our extremely serious views of promptness and doing things "on time." This is viewed by some as having led to a loss of quality both in a way of living and/or in the products of our efforts.

Yet within our national boundaries live people whose culture does not exert the same kind of press of time. For example, in the more traditional part of the South as well as in many rural farming and fishing communities in various parts of the country, a more relaxed attitude toward time may be found. This is not to say that promptness is not important in these places; it is just a different kind of promptness. It is the promptness of milking the cows at the appropriate time, planting in time to take full advantage of the growing season, or dropping the fishing nets at a time and place to maximize the catch. This is not the continuously pressing kind of promptness that one finds in the rapidly paced industrial centers.

In addition, Hall has indicated that there are people, such as the Sioux, who had "no understanding" of what it was to be "late" or to "wait." This supposition is based on the finding that they had no single words for these concepts in their language and that they had to be taught how to tell time and what time was when it was decided that it would be beneficial to adjust to white culture.

However, it is important to note here that suppositions based primarily on the equivalency of vocabulary in two different languages can be misleading. For example, what may require only one word or gesture in one linguistic group might require several words, whole sentences, and/or gestures in another linguistic group. What people need to express verbally and frequently helps determine their vocabulary, which in turn helps to illustrate what is important in their lives, although not necessarily all their concepts. Eskimos have many words for the English word snow. Because their lives may depend on it, an Eskimo uses a word for snow that also communicates its exact condition or when it fell. To express what the Eskimos do in one of their words for snow would take several English words in a phrase or sentence. This does not mean "no understanding" of snow on the part of English-speaking people. A comparative analysis of vocabulary between languages is insufficient evidence on which to base a judgment about the differences in concepts held by the linguistic groups whose vocabulary is compared (Lewis and Massad, 1975; Massad, 1969; Massad, Yamamoto, and Davis, 1970). Also, Webb, Campbell, Schwartz, and Sechrest (1966) caution about interpreting information obtained by means of language alone, and special care should be exercised if the language is different from the one generally spoken by the group from which the information is collected. When language is the medium of communication, the message may be distorted from the beginning by the built-in fibers of the given language used.

Because time is so often taken for granted to mean what individuals in a given culture conceive of as time, we seldom think about what we are communicating by our uses of time. We use time *formally*, such as indicating dates and days in a calendar year. We also use time *informally* by saying, "Oh, it takes years to do that!" What we really mean is that it takes minutes, hours, weeks, or months. Then, there is the *technical* use of time, as illustrated by discussions of the different types of years of different lengths. Is it any wonder then that it takes an average child more than 12 years to master the concept of time?

Consider this conversation between a father and a child: "When will we leave for the circus?" Father replies, "In a little while." The child asks, "How long is a while?" "It's hard to say." "Well, is it five minutes?" asks the child. "Sometimes, but not in this case. It'll probably be about 15 minutes, but don't waste time asking questions. Just get ready or we'll be late." "Oh," says the child, giving up for the moment.

The adult answers were really no answers at all, merely elaboration of the original puzzle! Children must learn to master the many categories of time used within their culture, even when it is difficult to get an exact fix on what is meant. For example, not only is time *valuable* since we must not waste it, but also it is like a product, since it can be measured, lost, made up, bought, and sold! Time concepts can be very difficult to comprehend, but, nevertheless, they tell a lot.

SPACE TALKS

By structuring the available space, we do communicate, though typically unaware of so doing. Spatial changes give a tone to an interpersonal exchange, accent it, and, sometimes, even have a greater effect than the spoken word. As an illustration, the normal conversational distance between strangers is greater than between two very good friends and, if a stranger comes too close, the immediate effect is for the other person to take a few steps backward. We back up also if we find people, or what they are saying, disagreeable.

Closed doors, marked corridors, roped off seats in a theatre, controlled restrooms, and locked playgrounds also express messages; these communicate social control. In addition, the placement of furniture imparts information. Just recall the time you entered an office and had to walk some distance to reach the visitor's seat across the desk from the person you came to see. Obviously this person was important and held a great deal of power to have such a spacious office in which a commanding, aloof position could be held. How different it is to walk into a tiny cubicle of an office and be seated next to the person being visited. Clearly space speaks.

People have developed their sense of space, their territoriality, to an almost unbelievable extent. Yet it has not really been discussed much until recent years. Perhaps because of its wide viewing audience, television, more than the theatre or books, led us to express vocally what we have for years practiced—declaring our territory—but tried to ignore formally or publicly in the guise of good manners. Archie Bunker, the main character of the television program "All in the Family," stresses the possession of "his chair," and it is humorous to see and hear Archie when anyone dares to sit in his chair. Archie, like young children, is quite open in telling everyone what space is his and not to be occupied by others.

This is not to say that most adults do not express their territoriality in some way. A new wife is often annoyed enough to tell her husband about a mother or mother-in-law walking into the kitchen "as if it were her own." An avocational carpenter will explode at anyone's "messing around" the carefully measured wood and other materials in his or her workshop. Just look in the daily newspaper, and you find that battles are still being sporadically fought over boundaries. Literally thousands of experiences teach us, unconsciously and consciously, that space communicates.

As one travels abroad, startling variations can be observed in the ways in which space is handled. Spatial cues that have meaning in their own context are learned by people as they grow up in their culture. The feelings and associations that a member of one culture expresses almost invariably mean something else in another culture. The important thing is to find out what cue was responsible for creating the feelings imparted; the next step is to discover, if possible, whether or not an individual intended to express this feeling and the reaction it produced. However, discovering specific cues in a foreign culture is a difficult and laborious process. One is bombarded by a strange language, different odors, gestures, signs, and symbols. Nevertheless, the difference the effort to understand makes in people's attitudes toward you may well be worth it. Perhaps the quickest way to learn is to talk to people who have been involved and living in the foreign culture for some time. As Hall (1959) so aptly expressed it, "Getting over a spatial accent is just as important, sometimes more so, than eliminating a spoken one" (150).

It is also interesting to note that formal space patterns take on varying degrees of importance, depending on the culture. For example, in the United States no one direction generally takes precedence over another unless it is for technical or utilitarian reasons. However, in other cultures some directions are sacred or preferred: Navajo doors must face east, Moslem mosques are oriented toward Mecca, and in India the sacred rivers flow south. Yet positional value or ranking is of great importance in our lives, to such an extent that children fight over who will be "first." Furthermore, we have a tendency to emphasize equality and standardization. That is, when space is divided, we insist on the units being equal and uniform. How else would we be able to have mass production? Standardization of parts of a product permits the production-line approach to making automobiles, refrigerators, shoes, or houses. Indeed, space talks. Our very productivity and success, as measured in our terms, rest to a large extent on our space and time patterns.

SUMMARY

I have briefly explored the dimensions of our world: time and space. Although we have long been aware of time and space, the very nature of our awareness may have diverted us from an in-depth exploration or examination of these two very critical aspects of our being and culture. *Time and space are there. They always have been and always will be.* We take them for granted. We are aware of them but not in a formal, conscious way. And because we do not have a formal awareness of time and space, we assume that everyone perceives and uses them in the same ways that we do. How wrong we are!

Time and space can be as personal as the secrets we keep to ourselves and share with no one. Our concepts of time and space develop, grow, and change as we do. They are affected by our environment, physical and cultural, just as we are. And just as we are all unique beings in this world, so are others and their concepts of time and space.

Of course when groups of people share a common environment, language, and beliefs, the personal, unique attributes of individuals are overshadowed by what they have in common, their culture. Research (Segall, Campbell, and Herskovits, 1966) has shown that differences across cultures can be great enough to surpass the ever-present individual differences within cultural groupings. Therefore, the first step in understanding people from another culture is to study the ways in which they, as a cultural group, are different from us. Knowing how they view time and space is a key to unlocking the door of their culture. Once we understand their culture, we can then begin to understand them as individuals, imparting the same respect for them that we would like to receive from them.

In the following chapters is a wealth of information that will help you as teachers, parents, and others interested in children and their development. It is in childhood, beginning at the *time* when an individual first occupies *space* inside the mother, that the building of concepts and behaviors begins to take form. This is the beginning of being, the beginning of an individual in a culture and in the world as a whole. To understand and help a child develop requires an understanding of his or her respective culture and of the child as an individual within that culture. By being aware of variations in time and space concepts, as well as of how time and space are used within society and schools, we will be better able to help children grow, to grow in *time* and *space*.

Suggested Readings

Asimov, Isaac. *Of time, space, and other things.* New York: Avon Books, 1965.

   This compilation of essays by one of the foremost writers on science for the lay reader covers a variety of topics. Here are lucid, interesting discussions of peoples' attempts to measure time and control it, gravitation as not the strongest force in the universe, speculations on human mortality, and other topics about space and time.

Goffman, Erving. *Relations in public.* New York: Basic Books, 1971.

   The discussion of human behavior here focuses on the study of rules for co-mingling. Gestural cues and "informing" signs other than the written and spoken ones are explained in the context of human communication and social organization.

Heidegger, Martin. *Being and time.* New York: Harper & Row, 1972.

   This work represents the author's efforts to discover the meaning of being. He poses the basic metaphysical question: Why is there something rather than nothing at all? The investigation is carried out in terms of the tools with which humans are practically concerned and their basic situation in time and space.

Mehrabian, Albert. *Public places and private spaces.* New York: Basic Books, 1976.

   The author, an environmental psychologist, describes the subtle though powerful influences of our surroundings on our feelings, moods, and day-to-day activities. In addition to providing a unique look at the psychology of places, there are also many practical suggestions for changing our private environments to suit our personal needs.

Toffler, Alvin. *Future shock.* New York: Bantam, 1971.

   A remarkable volume about what is happening today to people and groups who are overwhelmed by change. The author vividly describes the emerging super-industrial world; tomorrow's family life; and the rise of new businesses, subcultures, life styles, and human relationships. The intent is to help readers survive their collision with tomorrow.

Toulmin, Stephen, and Goodfield, June. *The fabric of the heavens.* London: Hutchinson, 1961.

In this highly readable and illuminating text, the authors fix attention on people's conceptions of the universe and their associated ideas about the way in which things move. Presented stage by stage is the 2,500-year-long intellectual argument, beginning with the Babylonian astronomers and ending with the basic picture of the solar system that we have today.

*In the far-ranging discussion that follows, an
educational psychologist probes the shape of
children's life space and its vicissitudes over time. We
look at the young with him but, paradoxically, what
we see is ourselves. By studying them, we come to
know us. Only through a deeper understanding of the
mystery of life in general can we hope to be of any
assistance to those whom we profess to guide.*

As Children See It

DAVID H. BAUER*

Down through the ages mankind has awakened "in a world that he
does not understand, and that is why he tries to interpret it" (Jung,
1940, p. 81). From their primordial consciousness the early Greeks
built elaborate symbol systems (myths, epic poems, art forms) to
give meaning to an unknown universe. Likewise during the Age of
Enlightenment Immanuel Kant emerged to give symbolic form to
the very foundations of the Western scientific world view by casting
modern man as an element suspended in a matrix of time, space,
and causality. Today the mystery of life remains, for humanity portrays itself as a lonely traveler aboard a tiny planet hurtling
through infinite three-dimensional space, coming from a dimly il-
luminated past, and going toward an uncertain future.

Yet in every generation human awareness is born anew, and that
awareness undergoes an ontogenetic (individual) development that
may partially reconstruct the phylogenetic (collective) history of

*I wish to express appreciation to Vicki T. Ross, California State University, Chico,
California, for her suggestions regarding an earlier version of this chapter and to
my sons, Jon and Kris, for sharing their views of time and space with me.

21

human consciousness (Bertalanffy, 1965; Cassirer, 1944) while giving form to an image of space and time in the firmament of life (Teilhard de Chardin, 1964). Said in another way, through the lives of its children humanity remembers its past, realizes its present, and shapes its future.

How, then, do children see the world of space and time? What do we know of the character of their understandings and perceptions as they grow to adulthood? How do they use these understandings to fashion their lives? Of what importance to children are the culturally transmitted mechanisms for organizing space and time? What do children's fantasies mean to the space and time of childhood?

I hope that as readers journey with children in the inner realm of time and space they may come to a deeper understanding of themselves as well as of those they teach.

IMAGE IN THE SAND OF TIME

"Human experience," said Bettelheim (1967), "is built upon our sense of time, space, and causality, Kant's *a priori* categories of mind" (p. 52). These categories are not simply speculative, for there seems to be an orderly sequence in which they appear in experience. As each individual life unfolds, a stable image of space seems to be structured out of the constant flux of momentary sensory experiences (Erikson, 1963; Piaget, 1954; Werner, 1957), and that organization is used to order time into past, present, and future. Let us, then, trace first the development of children's perception of, and relations to, space as they grow from the early to later years of childhood.

Division of the Firmament

Just as the Bible instructs that in the beginning space was given form before time, so child study teaches that children apprehend space before they conceive of time as a dimension of experience. Studies indicate, for example, that in the acquisition of language, spatial expressions appear before temporal ones, so that when asked a question such as, "When did the boy jump the fence?" three-year-olds tend to respond with such answers as "there" or "right there" (Clark, 1973). Such misinterpretation of "when" questions for "where" questions points to the fact that the organization of space precedes the ordering of time.

Likewise clinical observations reveal that emotionally disturbed children, who seem to have regressed to, or fixated at, early developmental stages, achieve a concept of space before they perceive a time dimension distinctly. In the following excerpt, for instance, Bettelheim (1967) portrays in dramatic form the failure to understand time in the experience of severely arrested schizophrenic and autistic children:

> Their day, for example, when it finally becomes ordered, is not organized in terms of morning, noon, and night, nor their space in terms of the location of rooms. Instead, a space-time concept is acquired rather early and given misleading names like "dining room" or "school." These concepts cover a unitary experience comprising both the time of day when they go from the dormitory to the dining room or the classroom and the movement through space required to get to these places. This they show by many types of behavior, one of which may illustrate: "School" to them means the time of day they go there, the place, and the person of their teacher. A holiday is "no school," and this throws them into severe panic: if they do not go to the usual place at the usual time, they are lost. Their space-time orientation does not work. (p. 53)

For these troubled children, temporal experiences are obviously equated with spatial ones, and their perceptions have the appearance of being bound to specific concrete experiences. As is often the case in child study, however, such close examination of special cases uncovers generalities common to the development of all children. Thus, though relatively little is known about the perception of space below about three years, studies of the development of space perception in normal children, as well as clinical observations of disturbed children, describe the appearance of spatial perceptions that are bound up with children's sensory and motor activities before the manifestation of more abstract representations of space.

Building Castles in the Sand

Werner (1957), for example, concluded from his studies of spatial perception that prior to the emergence of any highly abstract or visualized space, the perception of space is derived from the way things are physically handled. Similarly, after studying children's conceptions of space at varying age levels, Piaget and Inhelder (1956) offered the following summary of their observations regarding understandings in the early (sensorimotor), contrasted with later, stages.

> The space of the first period ... is ... one which is, above all else, completely egocentric in the sense that perceived relationships are not distinguished from the activity of the subject himself. (p. 12)

To illustrate, when Piaget and Inhelder asked two-year-old children to identify by visual inspection common objects such as spoons, keys, combs, and so forth, they were able to label them correctly. On the other hand, when asked to recognize the same objects by feeling and touching (tactile sensations) but not seeing them, a task that obviously demands imagining a visual representation from tactile impressions, the two-year-olds were unable to do so. By the age of three, however, the children studied were able to reconstruct the shapes of objects from tactile sensations, as evidenced by the fact that when familiar objects were hidden from sight, the older children recognized them simply by touching around the edges.

These results show that, below about three years of age, children begin to organize a spatial dimension of experience based largely on visual impressions. By age three, however, it appears that this organization becomes somewhat independent of direct visual signals from the environment, for children are able to synthesize abstract images from tactile sensations derived from touching the edges of objects. In general a close association exists between physical mobility (touching, manipulating, climbing) and a child's construction of a more abstract view of space. Through touching, holding on to, and letting go of people, places, and things, children build an imaginary world. To underscore the significance of the child's use of mobility in the construction of this reality, Montessori (1969) commented this way:

> If you watch a child of three, you will see that he is always playing with something. This means that he is working out, and making conscious, something that his unconscious mind had earlier absorbed. Through this outward experience, in the guise of a game, he examines those things and impressions that he has taken in unconsciously. He

becomes fully conscious and constructs the future man, by means of his activities. . . . In this way, he becomes a man. He does it with his hands, by experience, first in play and then through work. The hands are the instruments of man's intelligence. (p. 27)

Investigations (Werner, 1957) reveal, however, that with each advancing year of life children's spatial representations become progressively more independent of sensory stimulation from the external environment, so that even the toddler is not simply an organism reacting to physical stimuli from an objective world or acting upon its environment with the guidance of momentary signals. Rather, "He is oriented toward knowing, toward the construction of objects which mediate between him and his physical milieu. Whereas sensorimotor action is marked by a relative lack of differentiation between signal and action, cognition is marked by the . . . construction of symbols representing such things and events" (Wapner, Cirillo and Baker, 1971, pp. 163-164).

The Builders and Their Tools

Despite the fact that at an early age children begin to use symbols to represent objects and events in their life-space, readers should take care not to presume that a separation exists between children and their world, or between the objective and subjective in human knowledge. In the conception of science prevailing in modern American culture the tendency is to assume that there exists a basic dualism between self and world, an antithesis between body and mind, matter and soul, and object and subject. (For an extended discussion of the origin of this dichotomy and its manifestations in man's image of himself, see Yamamoto, 1977). While this assumption of ontological dualism is regarded by many as fundamental reality (Bertalanffy, 1965), it may lead easily to misunderstandings of children whose knowledge of the world is more personal. In fact, while the current conception of science focuses attention on the separation of the knower (subject) from the known (object), children's knowledge exists not separate from, but as an extension of, themselves in space (Polanyi, 1967).

To elaborate, in his discussion of the limitations to knowing inherent in the dualistic world view adopted by science in the twentieth century, Polanyi (1958, 1967) argued that instead of a separation, a fusion of self and world takes place in the act of knowing. According to him, just as young children use tactile impressions (mobility) to guide them in the construction of imaginary representations of objects, so do they continue to use the experience of their senses (termed *subsidiary* awareness) as clues for discovering an objective reality that transcends their sensory experience. These clues enable them to embrace a vision of a reality existing beyond the impression of their senses (termed *focal* attention). While such an account of the discovery of objective reality would be generally shrugged aside by modern science, it was precisely on this conception of objectivity that Polanyi insisted. He reasoned that into every act of knowing there enters a passionate contribution of the person knowing what is known, and this contribution is no imperfection but rather a vital component of his knowledge.

For example, in describing human use of physical objects as instruments for discovering (probes) and acting on (tools) their world, Polanyi (1958) clarified the nature of the extension of the self in space, which is an essential component of knowing:

> Our subsidiary awareness of tools and probes can be regarded . . . as the act of making them form a part of our own body. The way we use a hammer or a blind man uses his stick, shows in fact that in both cases we shift outwards the points at which we make contact with the things that we observe as objects outside ourselves. While we rely on the tool or probe, these are not handled as external objects. We may test the tool for its effectiveness or the probe for its suitability, e.g., in discovering the hidden details of a cavity, but the tool or probe can never lie in the field of these operations; they remain necessarily on our side of it, forming part of ourselves, the operating person. We pour ourselves out into them and assimilate them as part of our own existence. We accept them existentially by dwelling in them. (p. 59)

What, then, does Polanyi's seemingly esoteric thesis regarding personal knowledge mean to teachers? First, it means that to know a child a teacher must dwell in the life-space of that individual. While reliance on alleged "objective" descriptions of children offered by tools such as test scores, ratings on various scales, competencies on classroom tasks, and the like may satisfy the canon of modern science, such practices by themselves do not lead to a deeper understanding of the ineffable reality presented by a child. "A teacher will never succeed in giving proper guidance to a child if he does not learn to understand the psychological world in which that child lives. To substitute for that world of the individual, the world of the teacher, of the physicist, or of anybody else is to be, not objective, but wrong" (Lewin, 1951, p. 62).

Furthermore, acquiring personal knowledge demands that teachers not be preoccupied with filling children's minds with so-called "objective" facts. While a culturally enriched environment is a necessary condition for learning, the synthesis of personal knowledge demands that children be more than passive recipients of symbols representing objects and events in the physical universe. For them to discover reality personally and to create the necessary imaginary worlds, they need the freedom and opportunity to use such symbols in acting purposefully on their past (memory) and present experiences.

As an example, consider Robert Louis Stevenson's use of a deceptively simple symbolic representation, a map, in the creation of his classic book, *Treasure Island*.[1]

> I have said that the map was the most of the plot. I might almost say it was the whole. A few reminiscences of Poe, Defoe, and Washington Irving, a copy of Johnson's *Buccaneers*, the name of the Dead Man's Chest from Kingsley's *At Last*, some recollections of cannoeing on the high seas, and the map itself, with its infinite, eloquent suggestion, made up the whole of my materials. . . . The tale has a root there; it grows in that soil; it has a spine of its own behind the words. Better if the country be real, and he has walked every foot of it and knows every milestone. But even with imaginary places, he will do well in the beginning to provide a map; as he studies it, relations will appear that he had not thought upon; he will discover obvious, though unsuspected, shortcuts and footprints for his messengers; and even when a map is not all the plot, as it was in *Treasure Island*, it will be found to be a mine of suggestion. (p. xvi)

Stevenson's strikingly *purposeful use* of the map pointed him in the direction for discovery of this now legendary tale. In like manner, words, graphs, maps, and symbols in general are always point-

---

[1]The special edition of *Treasure Island* from which this quotation is taken was printed in 1941 by Heritage Press of New York.

ers toward the things they represent and are never the object of attention themselves. As Polanyi noted often, if attention is shifted from the meaning of a symbol to the symbol viewed as an object in itself, its meaning is destroyed. Just as skillful use of a tennis racket can be paralyzed by watching the racket instead of attending to the ball and court in front, so can a word such as "table" become a mere empty sound if repeated 20 times over. In general Polanyi (1959) emphasized that, "Symbols can serve as instruments of meaning only by being known subsidiarily while fixing . . . focal attention on their meaning" (p. 30).

Therefore, teachers or any other adults should not be surprised at all to find frustration and confusion when they demand that children focus on rote memorization and meaningless verbalization. In one incident I recall, our nine-year-old son, Kris, was required by his teacher to recite each of the multiplication tables from 2 to 12, devoting one minute for recitation of each. In the past, Kris had always been encouraged to take the time necessary to reason through an answer to any number combination not recognized immediately on presentation, so that a problem like 3×4 was understood to be the summation of three 4s or vice versa. With the imposition of the time pressure, Kris was forced into rote recall of meaningless numeric representations, and he confided to me that he was unhappy with school and disenchanted with his teacher after only three days in class.

Figures in the Sand

Up to this juncture I have said that, beginning in the early years, children use symbolic representations to organize a life-space from the transient and formless sense impressions making up at least part of their experience. Now the forms this symbolic representation of sensory experience may manifest as children develop into the later stages of childhood will be examined.

To begin, recall for the moment the fact that even young children are able to reconstruct the form of common objects by feeling and touching around their edges. Since the use of edges (perimeters) to structure perceptions agrees with the concerns of a particular branch of mathematics known as *topology,* the first discernible pattern in children's representations of space is called topological in nature.

The topology of space

Carrying further this thesis of an underlying topology in the child's representations of space, studies show that children begin to organize their world spatially by first defining the boundaries of situations as a whole. Only after this initial definition do various aspects and parts of the figures or objects undergo more detailed and refined analysis (Lewin, 1951). Laurendeau and Pinard (1970), for instance, found that between the ages of three and six years children are able to recognize from tactile sensations increasingly more abstract and detailed geometric forms. Initially figures having very elementary topological forms such as closed [Ⓞ] and open [Ⓢ;Ⓒ] rings are discriminated from one another, while shapes having the same borders but slightly different topological configurations, such as a closed ring and a disk with two holes [Ⓔ], are confused. At a later time children are able to differentiate among figures having such similar topological forms. Furthermore, even though older children are additionally able to recognize objects in projective (straight line, left-right, front-behind, etc.) and Euclidian (equidistantly spaced points, area, volume, etc.) relationships, the topology remains the fundamental scheme from which these more abstract relationships among parts of the whole perceptual field are derived (Sauvy and Sauvy, 1974).

As a case in point, consider the development of the child's comprehension of spatial perspective (projective relationship). Recognition of perspective requires that a person have the ability to coordinate his or her personal view with the view perceived when one projects oneself to another part of space. For instance, "A child who is able to distinguish perfectly well between his right and left is incapable of indicating correctly the left and right of someone facing him" (Sauvy and Sauvy, 1974, p. 26). To recognize perspective a child needs to integrate his or her personal point of view with the imagined perception of another individual occupying a separate position in space. To achieve such an integration, it is essential that the child perceives the situation as a whole with accompanying differentiated parts. Only by perceiving the parts in relation to the whole can individual elements (views of space) be coordinated with one another. Thus, the integration of views from varying points in space (perception of perspective) is made possible by understanding the parts in relation to the whole topological structure from which these parts are differentiated.

Now, let me digress for a moment to reflect on the broader significance of these facts. Recall that as the child seeks to comprehend perspective, the views from separate parts are understood by their relation to the whole perceptual field. The converse does not obtain. That is, simply reducing the whole to elemental parts does not lead the child to perceive perspective. More generally, the whole of experience is greater than the sum of its parts. It is a functioning totality whose parts enter into wholeness but cannot explain it.

Hence educators should not expect either to understand children or to lead them toward discovery of meaning in knowledge by reducing the dynamic totality represented by a life in progress to its constituent parts. While attempts at reducing the dynamic flow of life to static elemental units may accomplish the dissection of experience (termed *reductionism*) demanded by our analytic age (Eiseley, 1957), they do not help a child to discover meaning in his or her own existence. Nor do they encourage teachers to probe the deeper recesses of the total dynamic personalities developing in their classrooms rather than to focus on singular facets of surface behavior. Unfortunately the current curriculum movement stressing rigid sequencing of hierarchically organized information in competency/performance-based programs, as well as other school practices, reflects a powerful trend toward reductionism in American culture. Therefore, it is critical for teachers to keep in mind that just as children learn to comprehend spatial perspective by actively examining parts in relation to the whole, so too does school curriculum acquire meaning and become comprehensible only when analyzed by a child in relation to the whole of his or her individual and collective life experience.

Returning now to manifestations of the process of increasing articulation of a basic topology in the child's construction of spatial perceptions, this fundamental organizational scheme is reflected not only in the recognition of common objects but in the child's own productions as well. Consider, for instance, the series of drawings spontaneously created by one of my own children at progressively older ages (Figures 1 through 4). In the first drawing (Figure 1), which was constructed when Jon was about three years old, series of curvilinear figures circumscribe the boundaries of several separate entities, while two inner forms seem to differentiate the presence of "eyes" in an undifferentiated inner mass symbolized by scribbles. Worthy of note is that Jon constructed the boundary of each figure *before* adding interior details. When queried about these forms, Jon responded by saying that they were "ghosts."

Some months later he created the drawings depicted in Figure 2. Notice that, while the fundamental topological character remains with curvilinear lines defining the borders of significant features, straight lines are included, suggesting the separation of a head from torso.

At about age four Jon completed the drawings shown in Figure 3. Even greater differentiation of the earlier topology is reflected in this construction, as evidenced by the inclusion of a horizontal line representing a mouth, the addition of a third circular figure indicating the presence of a nose, and by the use of distinct vertical lines to describe a clear separation of the head from the legs of the figure.

Furthermore, the drawing depicted in Figure 4, which was completed shortly after the productions in Figure 3, evidences the addition of more detailed features such as the representation of a belt, which seems to differentiate a torso from the legs of the figure. In addition, a series of curvilinear and rectilinear lines adjacent to the main figure represent alphabetic letter formations. Such letters are commonly found in children's drawings at about age four (Kellogg, 1970), and, in this case, Jon alluded to the symbolic significance of the letters when he stated that the letters "say that he is a policeman."[2] In that regard, Jon noted that the circular figure on the hat of the man represents a "badge," further substantiating the symbolic character of this graphic production.

In sum, though the foregoing sequence of pictures spans a short

---

[2]Interestingly, a reviewer noted that, "My two-year-old grandson calls writing, 'O-E-O.' He says, 'I want to O-E-O,' meaning, 'Give me a crayon, I want to write.' Imagine my surprise when looking at Figure 4 to find the author's child writing O-E-O's to stand for the policeman. There must be something magical about O-E-O!" Indeed, regardless of the special meaning a particular symbol carries for any given child, the process remains the same. Symbols are used to give form to past and present experience and to shape future reality consciously.

Figure 1: Age Three

Figure 2: Age Three

Figure 3: Age Four

Figure 4: Age Four

time period in the life of a single child, the articulation of this topology in the structure of such deceptively simple products as figure drawings bears witness to children's purposeful use of symbols to differentiate perceptions. Children use symbols not merely to represent static perceptions but also to construct and control reality actively. Thus, at about age five, Jon spontaneously paged through the series of drawings shown in Figures 1 through 4 and labeled each as representing either "ghosts" or "cops." After proudly reviewing his past works, he revealed the constructive nature of his symbolic creations when he tellingly said, "The cops *killed* the ghosts!" Both literally and figuratively, Jon's later symbolic constructions ("cops") put an end to ("killed") his earlier global perceptual representations ("ghosts"). Interestingly, at younger ages children generally tend to refer to these same global representations ("ghosts") when asked about what they are most afraid of and about frightening dreams they experience (Bauer, 1976).

In any case, between about five and twelve years of age, the character of the representative function seems to undergo fundamental alterations which, in turn, appear to be reflected in children's understanding of their relationship to others and to objects in space.

Concrete versus abstract figures

To be more specific, between about four and seven years of age, representations tend to retain elements of egocentrism and do not seem to distinguish between objects signified and the symbols used to represent them (Piaget and Inhelder, 1956).[3] Moreover, the egocentric character of their perceptions is reflected in the fact that they do not appear to differentiate between their personal perspectives and the points of view held by others. Despite the fact that younger children use signs to stand for objects and events, early in life "the name or other symbol . . . not only represents, but is the reality in question" (Bertalanffy, 1965, p. 56). As a result, rather than structuring new images, or anticipating experiences, the rep-

---

[3]The reader should take care not to confuse the concept of *egocentrism*, which refers to children's tendency not to distinguish their own from others' perceptions, with the notion of *egotism*, which describes a more general self-centeredness and indifference to the concerns of others.

resentations of the young child often simply state perceptions (Piaget and Inhelder, 1956).

Thus, Laurendeau and Pinard (1970) found that while children of six or seven years of age can recognize visual representations (line drawings) of complex geometric figures from tactile perceptions, they have difficulty imagining which one of several pictures taken of the same scene from varying perspectives in space represents the view of a person stationed at vantage points differing from their own. Only at a later stage of development (about age nine or ten) did the majority of children use symbols to imagine the objective view of another and, thereby, to coordinate their own perspective with that of another individual occupying a different location in space.

Coordinating a personal view of objects in space with perspectives of others demands that children use symbols to differentiate experience into three separate parts, namely, one that appears in space as a unique self, labeled the *I*, another, inanimate portion that seems to be separate from that self, referred to as the *It*, and finally a component that makes up the collective experience of other animate beings, termed the *Thou* (Bertalanffy, 1965). In other words, through symbolic representations children crystallize out of the flow of undifferentiated experience a spatial world comprised of *I*, *Thou* and *It*. "The I," however, "grasps itself through its counterpart in verbal action, and only as this latter becomes more established and sharply defined, does the I truly find itself and understand its unique position" (Cassirer, 1953, p. 277).

Faces in the sand

Not surprisingly, as they grow older children establish around themselves a series of spatial spheres, or *personal space* zones, which define the physical distances maintained in various types of verbal and nonverbal encounters with others (Hall, 1959, 1970). More specifically, through essentially four concentric circles delimiting intimate, personal, social, and public areas of interpersonal space, children represent in terms of distance in physical space their inner feelings about other people as well as about themselves. As a result, despite the fact that the psychosocial dynamics contributing to the development of personal space zones are not understood fully and that the relationship between physical and psychological distances is not perfect, by the time children reach about age nine, an inverse relationship appears between the amount of physical distance children place between themselves and others and the degree of liking of, and acquaintance with, those people (Meisels and Guardo, 1969).

The presence of an inverse relationship between physical distance and psychological distance in personal space is of special importance to teachers, for studies show that children identified as "emotionally disturbed" (Weinstein, 1965) as well as "disruptive" boys (Fisher, 1967) tend to place greater physical distance between figures representing significant others, such as parents and teachers, than do more normal children. Unfortunately, rather than defining themselves through a relationship of the *I* with the *Thou*, it appears that children who are already separated from others reject, withdraw from, and distrust those with whom they might search for inner peace. As a consequence of such self-isolation, not only does the *I* doubt the *Thou*, but it mistrusts itself and fails to establish its uniqueness. Writing on the difficulty disturbed children have in defining themselves in relation to others, Moustakas (1959) commented this way:

> At the root of the child's difficulty is the submission and the denial of his self. Somewhere along the line of his growth and development, he has given up the essence of his being and the unique patterns that distinguish him from every other person. The growth of the self has been impaired because of his rejection in important personal relationships. He has been severely rejected by others and he has come to reject himself. He is cut off from his vital self-resources which would enable him to develop in accordance with his own particular talents. (pp. 3-4)

Investigations reveal that economically disadvantaged children also remove themselves psychologically from the group, including that group they identify as being most like themselves (Tolor and Orange, 1969). Similarly, young children who experience difficulty separating from their mothers show a pattern of general withdrawal and rejection. Leach (1972), for example, found that preschool-age children having trouble separating directed less behavior toward, and were less responsive to, other three-, four-, and five-year-olds in their nursery school. Correspondingly, the other children interacted less with them than with each other. Unfortunately the paradoxical situation also existed in which, even though the troubled children remained close to their mothers, they were less responsive to them than was normal, while the mothers themselves tended to avoid interactions with their children.

To sum up, the use of symbols makes possible the synthesis of an abstract spatial universe differentiated into objective and subjective dimensions. Children use these symbols to understand their place in space and to define the relation of their selves to others and to objects in space. There is need to recognize, however, that since these dimensions are abstractions from the totality of experience, they do not constitute the whole of mankind's being.

Symbolism provides the vehicle through which children not only comprehend themselves in space but also order their immediate experience according to temporal categories. Thus, continuity is brought to an otherwise momentary awareness of abstract space. Bertalanffy (1965), for example, made these remarks about the function of symbolism in the creation of a time dimension in human consciousness:

> It is the representative function which creates a "universe." Immediate experience, such as perception of things, feelings, acts of will, and so forth, is momentary—dominating consciousness at one moment and gone the next. . . . Only when symbolism arises does experience become an organized "universe." Only then do past and future exist in their symbolic images, thereby becoming manageable. The past becomes part of the organized universe; the future can be anticipated by way of its symbolic stand-ins, and so can determine actual behavior. Thus, symbolism makes for the consistency of the universe. (p. 57)

SAND THROUGH THE HOURGLASS

What do studies reveal about changes in children's understandings of time as they mature from infancy to adulthood? Is any developmental sequence discernible in the child's organization of experience into past, present, and future? How do strategies for organizing individual life-times into temporal units such as days, weeks, months, and years originate in children's awareness? Of what significance in children's lives are these linearly arranged, hierarchically ordered temporal structures?

"The small child lives in the present," observed Lewin (1951), "his time perspective includes only the immediate past and the immediate future" (p. 75). But with increasing age the child's perspective on time grows to include more and more distant future and past. Out of their increasingly abstract understandings of spatial relationships, children in American culture synthesize an image of time based on their vision of space (Clark, 1973). Just as they learn to see themselves as existing separately from objects and others in space, so do they come to perceive time as something that is outside themselves, that is arranged linearly into past, present, and future, and through which they are projected on the way from birth to death (Kluckhohn and Strodtbeck, 1961).

Rhythm of Life, Tempo of Time

Prior to the emergence of any abstract conception of time, however, children's understandings are grounded in more concrete sensory experiences. During infancy, for example, natural internal physiological rhythms such as heartbeat, electrochemical activity of the brain, and breathing tempo are harmonized with the periodicity in occurrences outside the child such as feeding times, activity periods associated with day and night cycles, occasions of parental fondling, and the like. This fundamental connection between inner and outer worlds seems to be reflected in the view of time carried into adulthood.

Cross-cultural investigations reveal that the pattern in parental handling of children's basic physiological and emotional needs during the first year of life is reflected in the conception of time prevalent among adults in varying world cultures. For example, Zern (1970) demonstrated that those cultures in which caretakers engage in less indulgent child-rearing in the first year exhibit a more highly structured and salient sense of time than do cultures in which child-rearing is more nurturant. In conducting his study Zern rated cultures on (1) dimensions of nurturance such as offering protection from environmental discomforts, constancy of presence of the nurturing agent, and consistency and degree of drive (e.g., hunger, thirst, unidentified discomforts) reduction, and on (2) the saliency of their time concepts. An indication of a high degree of saliency was evidenced in features such as a developed calendar of a year in length, a break-up of the month into different segments (e.g., weeks), a naming of particular days of the week or month, and so forth. Conversely, a low degree of saliency was marked by a lack of such features. Interestingly, Zern discovered an inverse relationship between the amount of nurturance in cultures and the degree of saliency and structure in their conception of time.

Evidently a minimal amount of indulgence is a biological essential and is found in all cultures. Nonetheless, adults communicate much of the particular temporal order in the culture by their differential handling of gratification of the needs of infancy. Cultures having hierarchically organized, elaborately structured, and salient temporal organizations seem to encourage children to begin to structure their inner world by mildly frustrating needs early in life. In contrast, cultures having less differentiated time perspectives appear to be more indulgent of demands for immediate gratification of children's basic needs.

Images of Yesterday, Today and Tomorrow

From the foregoing discussion, it can be seen that the child first becomes oriented to time through the cyclic activities bearing a concrete relationship to the rhythms of life, and these recurring personal events in the child's life form the basis for more abstract understanding of past, present, and future. From his comprehensive review of the literature, Fraisse (1963) concluded that by 18 months of age, children can imagine events such as a "bath" and a "visit to grandmother's house," which occurred regularly in the past and are anticipated to recur in the near future. By age two, many children are capable of recalling memories from about a month ago, while they begin to make reference to more distant, but periodic, future events such as "tomorrow" and "this afternoon." At three years, children already appear to have memories from as much as a year before, and at five these recollections may go back two years. By the time they reach four years, they refer to cyclic events of even longer duration such as the seasons of the year ("next summer") and important festival events (Christmas or birthday), and by five years these references may be relatively precise.

In general, as they grow and develop, children abstract from their immediate personal experience symbolic images of yesterday, today, and tomorrow, and developmental changes in the structure of these more imaginary forms of understanding show a topological organization reminiscent of the structure in children's spatial representations. Just as children first organize their spatial perceptions by defining the boundaries of figures or objects as a whole before differentiating details, so too do they initially delimit the edges of time in their perceptual field before identifying periods making up intervals of longer and shorter duration.

To be more precise, while it is true that the first words used by children in dealing with time refer to frequently recurring cycles involving personal activities (birthdays, holidays, and so on), these early verbal signs tend to be egocentric. As the reader may recall, these symbols are not distinguished from the actions they represent. After age five, however, less egocentric representations progressively appear. In a study of school-age children's understanding of time, Bradley (1947) found that the "day" is understood first. Knowledge of shorter and longer periods follows. For example, Bradley pointed out that prior to differentiating time into periods shorter than one day (minutes, hours, seconds, morning, afternoon), children comprehend the week, followed by the month, and subsequently the year. Interestingly, Bradley concluded from his study that the most difficult aspect of time for children to comprehend was the concept of duration.

Before going on, allow me to comment on the primacy of an understanding of the "day" in children's perceptions of time from a personal experience with our youngest son, Jon, who at the time of the story was four years old. Whenever an agreement was reached that we were to make a trip to a local ice cream store for a treat we both enjoyed very much, I made a statement implying duration such as "later on today," "this afternoon," or "in a little while." Jon responded by saying, "No, Dad, today! Today, Dad! Let's go today!" His emphasis was always on the word "today." If, in an attempt to improve our verbal communication, I said, "After we have lunch, Jon," my reference to a discrete temporal point ("lunch") rather than to duration ("later on") seemed to clarify for Jon exactly when we were to go.

In another incident Jon repeatedly questioned the anticipated time of our arrival at our destination of a trip lasting several days. In trying to explain that our drive would take several more "days" (duration), such statements as, "We shall be at grandmother's house in three days" met with little genuine comprehension, as evidenced in responses such as "Oh . . . ?" Likewise, my references to nights to be spent in motel rooms contributed little to his understanding, and it was not until the morning of the day of our arrival that Jon seemed to comprehend that, "*Today* we shall be at grandmother's house."

In any case, when they reach about age eight, children are capable of envisioning plans for the future outside the limits of customary activities in their daily lives, as evidenced in the fact that they begin to show concern for their life as an adult by making statements such as "I shall get married," "I shall be a physician," "I want to be a baseball player when I grow up," and so forth. The first images of the future beyond childhood, however, seem to be largely free from the constraints imposed by a conception of time in which the future is perceived as spatially separated from the present along a linear extension. As a result, children of middle and later childhood age tend to have available to them an image of the future for the fulfillment in imagination of what seems to adults to be in reality unrealizable desires. To illustrate, in his study of the time perspectives of maladjusted contrasted with normal 10- to 17-year-olds, Klineberg (1967) discovered that maladjusted preadolescents (10- to 12-year-olds) were more oriented toward what he termed the "distant future" (adulthood) than were emotionally healthy ones. Maladjusted adolescents, on the other hand, tended to constrain their subjective vision of this linearly "remote future."

From the results of his study Klineberg concluded that, since preadolescents tend to perceive their future less in terms of linear distance in *space,* children who are frustrated and unhappy with themselves can project fantasies on their image of the future as an escape from the present condition of their lives. Conversely, since adolescents envision the future as separated from them along a linear *time* dimension, an image of the remote future is not used for fulfilling unrealizable desires. To make the situation somewhat distressing, while preadolescent children who are not maladjusted tend to be involved in the present rather than to focus on the future, this condition does not obtain among adolescents in emotional distress, for they not only limit their outlook on the future but also avoid involvement in present experience and perform poorly in school. For the majority of children, however, the transition from childhood to adolescence brings increased concern for present activities that promise gratification in a future that is perceived as removed from their present state but to which they are trajected on a linear course.

And so the die is cast. By the time they reach adolescence, children understand temporal succession and order by abstracting from experience a representation of themselves moving past a series of discrete locations in space (Clark, 1973). Moreover, "When [they] perceive succession, [they] apprehend at the same time an ordered multiplicity and the intervals separating the individual elements, that is to say, the durations. 'Duration is, as it were, the measure of the succession, the value of the interval.'" (Fraisse, 1963, p. 76). Out of their struggle to understand duration, then, children learn to represent time as a spatial metaphor in which they see themselves in movement past a series of discrete points making up the line marked by the trajectory of their self in space (Bergson, 1965; Clark, 1973; Kluckhohn and Strodtbeck, 1961). Furthermore, since duration is viewed by setting out in a line all past, present, and future events, children are encouraged to believe that their personal futures are derivable from the connection of various events in the series, that the goals of life need to be established early if they are to be attained, and that others, who are further along the path than they, should have primary responsibility for determining the course of their lives. Thus, children come to see their lives being controlled by forces outside themselves as they progress through a succession of linearly arranged temporal units.

But do children come to a true understanding of time by representing it as if it were space? Does their newly acquired cosmology guide them toward an understanding of the inner experience of time and of self, which these symbolic images merely represent?

In Search of Time and Self

In at least partial response to such a challenging metaphysical[4] question, Bergson (1965) indicated that throughout the ages of human consciousness, time has been represented as space, and, as a

---

[4]Metaphysics is the branch of philosophy that seeks to explain the origin of being (ontology) and the structure of the world (cosmology).

consequence, mankind understands the image of time but not time itself. He cautioned that for all of us, the elimination of time is a habitual, normal, commonplace act of our understanding. To gain a vision of the reality of time, he advised, "is not a question of getting outside of time (we are already there); on the contrary, one must get back into duration and recapture reality in the very mobility which is its essence" (p. 31). It follows that if mankind's use of signs to represent time eliminates the reality of time, then by abstracting from the same flow of inner experiences symbolic representations of *I, Thou* and *It*, humanity understands a differentiated image of reality rather than the inner reality itself. Further, since symbols describe discontinuous states instead of the dynamic movement of experience, children normally understand the static representations of experience rather than the inner reality to which these symbols give form. Thus, the nature of the real relationship of a child's inner life to his or her conceptions of self, others, and objects remains largely unknown and unexplored (Bergson, 1965).

Nevertheless, mankind has always been intuitively aware of the existence of a more fundamental inner reality as a naturally occurring part of life, and his tormented search for it is documented in the art, history, and literature of every generation. Through their dreams, poetry, music, and other nondiscursive symbolic forms,[5] children of every age seek to find a reality that lends continuity to what has come to be in their life (the past) and that which they promise to become in the future (Erikson, 1964). The struggle for discovery of that reality, termed by Jung (1940) as the *self* or *inner center,* is inevitably a long, lonely, often painful process.

For each person the questions, "Who am I?" and "Where am I going?" begin early and recur throughout life, and it is the careful listening for a response from within, instead of for an answer from without, that guides an individual toward psychological maturity and realization of the *self* (Franz, 1964). Consequently, rather than instructing children to fix a linear path toward remote utilitarian

---

[5]The reference here is to Bertalanffy's (1965) distinction between *discursive* and *nondiscursive* symbols. Generally speaking, *discursive* symbols are those that communicate facts, whereas *nondiscursive* symbols convey emotions and motivations. Nondiscursive symbols are represented at the higher levels in forms such as music, poetry, art, and so forth, all of which communicate intimate experience rather than objective thoughts.

goals established for them by significant adults, teachers need to help children cultivate in their lives the ability to listen intelligently to their own inner voices in their quest for a meaningful future. By interpreting communications originating from within, children may be led to fulfillment of their own identities rather than toward alienation of the conscious symbolic representation of their selves (their egos) from their own inner beings. Take, for instance, the following excerpt in which Wickes (1963) vividly portrays the anguished loss of *self* that may arise from excessive reliance on voices from without (e.g., financial success, social achievement, or prestige in the eyes of colleagues) instead of on the authentic voice of *self* in guiding their lifetime:

> The ego may disregard the demands of the Self, leaving behind the early visions, the promptings of the heart, the simple human claims, and forget that the soul is the one who acts as interpreter of the creative images that arise from the depth of our being. For a long time the loss of soul may go unnoticed, activities increase, acquisitions multiply, yet underneath the achievement nothing satisfies, nothing nourishes; there is only emptiness. To stop to look into the depth would reveal, not that nothingness of the void out of which all unborn things come into creation, but the bottomless void of meaninglessness. Still the ego presses on—one more step and the goal that consciousness has set will be reached and the restless ego can rest satisfied, then will come plenty of time for enjoyment, for relatedness to his fellow men, for self-reflection, for inwardness, for the discovery of meaning. But instead, moments of depression increase, life slips away like sand through Time's hourglass, and the man secretly fears that death may come before the moment of achievement when one really begins to live. Questions arise. Who am I? What am I seeking? What dreams of the morning are now lost in the dusk of oncoming night? How can I find that sense of life that my youth once knew? Perhaps in spite of the ego's disregard of all except its own effort to pull itself out of the slough by its own bootstraps, these restless questions may penetrate below the surface. (pp. 289-290)

Clearly the realization of one's personal destiny does not entail orientation toward goals established by others to be attained in a remote, but completely foreseeable, future. Rather, what seems to be necessary is that children be allowed to live fully in the present as they seek to fulfill their personal destinies in a tomorrow of which they have vision and in a future in which they have trust. Unfortunately in American culture the assumption is commonly made that children are motivated either by forces from without or by a desire to gratify some need by domination and willful action, and that belief discourages parents as well as teachers from allowing children to look for answers from sources inside, instead of outside, themselves. Since the tendency is to presume that the distant future can be foretold by virtue of its linear trajectory, teachers are led to believe that if they place activities in a linear sequence beginning in the present and extending into the future, they can assure a child of material success in his or her social world. As a consequence, children learn not to place trust in themselves or in their uncertain future; rather, they learn to rely on sources of power outside themselves to give direction and purpose to their lives. In general the inclination prevalent in the culture is not to recognize that psychological growth originates within the person and that, to be teachers in the truest sense, adults need to lead children to an inner strength by which they can face an unknown future "preserved and guarded, invulnerable, clad in the silver mail of trust" (Buber, 1965, p. 98).

That fundamental wisdom was expressed beautifully by Emily Dickinson who affirmed in her poetry the agony and the ecstacy that was hers in a lifetime search for self:

> Growth of Man—like Growth of Nature—
> Gravitates within—
> Atmosphere, and Sun endorse it—
> But it stir—alone—
>
> Each—its difficult Ideal
> Must achieve—Itself—
> Through the solitary prowess
> Of a Silent Life—
>
> Effort—is the sole condition—
> Patience of Itself—
> Patience of opposing forces—
> And intact Belief—
>
> Looking on—is the Department
> Of its Audience—
> But Transaction—is assisted
> By no Countenance—

Belief in Self, Trust in the Unknown

Intact belief—belief in life, belief in the *self,* trust in the unknown—that is the most significant achievement of life in the childhood years. By the prohibitions and permissions imposed by parents along with other significant adults, children are guided toward varying amounts of trust in themselves and in the unknown. On the fundamental relationship between inner trust and the outer cosmic ordering of time, Erikson (1963) wrote:

> The infant's first social achievement, then, is his willingness to let the mother out of sight without undue anxiety or rage, because she has become an inner certainty as well as an outer predictability. Such consistency, continuity, and sameness of experience provide a rudimentary sense of ego identity which depends, I think, on the recognition that there is an inner population of remembered and anticipated sensations and images which are firmly correlated with the outer population of familiar and predictable things and people. (p. 247)

From their earliest experiences, children structure images of the future distinguished by differing amounts of order, predictability, and controllability. Thus, children who experience dependable and continuous care imbued with warmth and who are allowed to exercise some control over their lives tend to depict the future as predictable, meaningful, and safe. Conversely, children who live with disorder, excessive restrictiveness or permissiveness, and hostility seem to become more distrustful of their world and of themselves. They simply have fewer experiences on which to base their expectations about life, through which to exert control over their fate, and from which to build belief in themselves and in their future.

Studies show that though the effects of parent-child relations are extremely complex, a number of consistent consequences of varying approaches to parental guidance are identifiable. For example, Becker (1964) reviewed the then available research and uncovered two bipolar dimensions of parental behavior, which he labeled *restrictive* vs. *permissive* and *warmth* vs. *hostility.* Figure 5, which is an adaptation of the highly informative summary appearing in Becker's article, depicts the influence of different styles of child-rearing.

Restrictiveness

Submissive, dependent, polite, neat, obedient Minimal aggression Maximum rule enforcement (boys) Dependent, not friendly, not creative Maximal compliance	"Neurotic" problems More quarreling and shyness with peers Socially withdrawn Low in adult role-taking Maximal self-aggression (boys)

Warmth ———————— **Hostility**

Active, socially outgoing, creative, successfully aggressive Minimal rule enforcement (boys) Facilitates adult role-taking Minimal self-aggression Independent, friendly, creative, low projective hostility	Delinquency Noncompliance Maximal aggression

Permissiveness

Figure 5. Child-rearing consequences of parental warmth vs. hostility and restrictiveness vs. permissiveness. (Constructed from Becker. 1964)

Study of Figure 5 reveals that children of permissive-hostile parents tend to absorb parental hostility and react to external events with aggressive impulses themselves (delinquency, noncompliance), while children reared in restrictive-hostile settings seem to internalize parental aggression by directing anger against themselves in the form of guilt (self-aggression) and anxiety (social withdrawal, neurosis, shyness with peers). On the other hand, as Becker (1964) pointed out, since children with "warm-permissive parents [are] socialized mainly through love, good models, reasons, and trial-and-error learning of how [their] actions (which are a bit uncontrolled at times) have an impact on others" (p. 198), they appear to approach life with optimism and trust in themselves.

For parents to offer good models, love, and reason does not, however, mean that they invariably behave in an affirmative, acceptant, and benign manner toward the child's every impulse and action. Excessively permissive parental behaviors have been found to be associated with greater amounts of aimlessness and suggestibility and lesser degrees of independence, purposiveness, and achievement orientation among children (Baumrind, 1973). On the other hand, rigidly authoritarian patterns of parenting, in which children's autonomy is restricted to assure obedience and to preserve order and tradition and in which verbal give-and-take is not encouraged, tend to generate child behaviors characterized by greater submissiveness than dominance, more hostility than friendliness, and more resistiveness than cooperation. Paradoxically, extremely authoritarian parenting appears to result in the same general lack of independence and achievement orientation as is found in children whose parents are excessively permissive.

What seems to be needed in parenting are behaviors that Baumrind (1973) categorized as *Authoritative*. According to her, "The *Authoritative* parent attempts to direct the child's activities in a rational, issue-oriented manner. Both autonomous self-will and disciplined conformity are valued by Authoritative parents; they affirm the child's present qualities but also set standards for future conduct. They use reason, power, and shaping by regime and reinforcement to achieve objectives" (p. 135). In general, authoritative parents view the control aspect of their parental role, including their role as disciplinarians who at times use punishment, as facilitative of competence and therefore independence in their offspring. Children of authoritative parents tend to be more cooperative, friendly, achievement oriented, independent, and dominant than they are resistive, hostile, suggestible, or submissive.

Regardless of child-rearing style, however, parents need to communicate genuine caring in their relationships with children, for the effects of a general lack of warmth in early interactions with children may be far-reaching. Take, for instance, the following case reported by Bühler (1968):

A case in point is that of Louise, a woman in her early thirties who in hypnosis recaptured three short episodes of experiences she had had with her mother at what, as was established later, must have been her tenth month of life.

In the first episode she saw herself sitting on the floor of the kitchen and looking at her mother, who seemed to be standing far away at the stove. She longed for her mother to turn toward her, but this did not happen.

Then she saw herself jumping up and down in her cradle looking for her mother and hoping she would come through the door. Nobody came.

In the third scene she saw herself in the arms of her mother, whose head was turned to talk to a neighbor. Louise again yearned for her mother to turn to her but in vain.

Waking up crying, Louise admitted that this was the way she had always felt, "being nothing at all" to her mother, just existing.

This feeling of worth or worthlessness, based on the feeling of being loved or unloved, probably contributes most to a person's or even already a child's sense of self.

Louise has suffered from a lack of confidence and from depression ever since she can remember. She became submissive in order to be accepted, she withdrew and resigned herself to being unable to obtain or achieve what she wanted. (p. 176)

Unmistakably, this troubled woman cried out for a dialogue with another human being very early in life, and the failure to commune with her "cold" mother undoubtedly contributed to the feelings of worthlessness and rejection that were part of her existential despair.[6] For all of us, the ". . . *I* and *Thou* exist only in our world, because man exists, and the *I*, moreover, exists only through the relation to the *Thou*" (Buber, 1965, p. 205). Between a human being and another, where *I* and *Thou* meet, there is the realm of the "between." In that reality our children can either establish a genuine sense of community and an unalterable faith in the *Self* and its future, or they can resort to self-absorption, despair, and hopelessness about their personal future as well as the collective fortune of mankind. Of special importance to those responsible for educating children, therefore, are the means through which children come to recognize the presence of that venerable reality and to believe in themselves and their future, despite the feelings of pain, isolation, loneliness, helplessness, and rejection that are an inexorable part of a growing life.

---

[6]It is important to note that studies show rather conclusively that the individuality of the child determines to a large extent his or her interpretation and use of any given situation (Caldwell, 1964) and that practitioners need to view ". . . the parent-child relation as an interactive system rather than one in which child behavior is a consequence of parental behavior" (Martin, 1975, p. 463).

MAGIC IN THE GOLDEN GLEAM

Closing his story, *Through the Looking Glass*, with this poem, Lewis Carroll expressed his intimate experience of a reality transcending the bounds of symbolized time and space and immortalized for mankind the wisdom in its dreams and fantasy:

A boat, beneath a sunny sky
Lingering onward dreamily
In an evening of July —

Children three that nestle near,
Eager eye and willing ear,
Pleased a simple tale to hear —

Long has paled that sunny sky:
Echoes fade and memories die:
Autumn frosts have slain July.

Still she haunts me, phantomwise,
Alice moving under skies
Never seen by waking eyes.

Children yet, the tale to hear,
Eager eye and willing ear,
Lovingly shall nestle near.

In a Wonderland they lie,
Dreaming as the days go by,
Dreaming as the summers die:

Ever drifting down the stream —
Lingering in the golden gleam —
Life, what is it but a dream?

"Life, what is it but a dream?" And children, what are they but the dreamers? Recall that out of the flow of undifferentiated life, the *I* is separated from the *Thou* as well as from the *It*, but that, early in life, these divisions are indistinct. That is, symbols tend not to be distinguishable from what they represent. Object (*It*) and subject (*I*) are inseparable. Personal perspectives (*I*) are found not to be differentiated from the points of view held by others (*Thou*). In psychological parlance, perceptions are said to be egocentric. Fantasy is said not to be differentiated from reality (Piaget, 1962).

Yes indeed, "Life, what is it but a dream?" Dreams and fantasy, they are the silvery mist in the looking glass through which, as if by magic, children see a dimension of life veiled by objective space and time. They are the fibers that bind children together in the face of growing separation and isolation in their individual lives. They are the threads that weave continuity in life, so that children can live today fully conscious of their yesterdays as they grow toward their tomorrows. They are the filaments that lead into the flow of time and down to the deeper source of life from which they tend to stray. They are the fabric on which chaotic feelings are woven into conscious form and in which children master emotions in order to build trust in an unknown future. Bearers of mystery in the truest sense, dreams and fantasy are a gift of magic, given so that mankind might find purpose rather than despair in its individual and collective life.

Gift of Magic, Legacy of Love

What are human beings? Where did they come from? Where are they going? From the earliest periods of human history, mankind has asked these questions, and cultures have turned to the power of fantasy to interpret the meaning of their existence (Toulmin and Goodfield, 1965). As a result, down through the centuries a treasure of nondiscursive symbols such as myths, folk ballads, poetry, and art forms of varying types have been passed from generation to generation to help each individual in the struggle with these essential questions (Murray, 1960). For children, however, a special collection of stories has evolved to be used in the search for meaning; these *folk fairy tales* are written in a language children understand and address the inner conflicts of childhood (Bettelheim, 1976). Tales such as "The Three Little Pigs," "Hansel and Gretel," "Little Red Riding Hood," "Snow-White," and "Sleeping Beauty" are familiar ones in Western culture, and they offer children a means for conceptualizing and controlling deep-rooted emotions such as powerlessness in an adult world, fear of abandonment by parents, and anger and rage stemming from life's frustrations and disappointments as well as other feelings.

Unfortunately, while much of the literature available to children in modern society represents the creative efforts of individual adults and is designed to inform and to develop skills usable in a remote future, little of it is directed at helping children find meaning in their daily lives by enriching it and giving conscious form to their emotions. The child, much more than the adult, lives in the present, is perplexed by feelings, and has only the vaguest notions of the distant past and future beyond his or her daily life. Yet most literature used in schools and homes merely amuses and entertains while attempting to communicate abstract images of people and things existing outside the borders of their life-space. It does not typically provide children with access to deeper meanings, which are to be found only in the rich literary heritage that has been transmitted by the collective experience of the culture. Speaking on the type of literature that helps children find meaning, Bettelheim (1976) wrote:

> For a story to hold a child's attention, it must entertain him and arouse his curiosity. But, to enrich his life, it must stimulate his imagination; help him to develop his intellect and to clarify his emotions; be attuned to his anxieties and aspirations; give full recognition to his difficulties, while at the same time suggesting solutions to the problems which perturb him. In short, it must at one and the same time relate to all aspects of his personality — and this without ever belittling but, on the contrary, giving full credence to the seriousness of the child's predicaments, while simultaneously promoting confidence in himself and in the future. (p. 5)

Literature that provides this genre of education stems not from the efforts of any single individual working in isolation, however. Rather it issues from the wisdom pervading the human group, from the realm that exists between one human being and another, from a state of collective human consciousness, from a sort of generalized human personality "which is inherited by each succeeding generation of conscious individuals, and to which each generation adds something" (Teilhard de Chardin, 1964, p. 33). The learning that arises from this heritage, moreover, pertains not to the being of the world transfixed as an object in time and space, but instead, to its being a subject in the present reality and its becoming in the future. Written by authors who remain unknown, stories known as folk fairy tales constitute a legacy of love, handed down so that children may be guided in the present as they dream of the future.

Take, for example, the fact that such stories consider the child's vague understanding of time by beginning with indefinite references to the past rather than to discrete temporal points, with phrases such as, "Once upon a time," "Many years ago," "Once long ago and far away," and so forth. By using such phrases, the stories begin by leading children away from their abstract representation of the past and guiding them back into the experience of time. More specifically, recall that the use of symbols removes us from the flow of time by creating static images of the past and future. The present, however, remains a mystery in which past and future are represented. Is not the present moment gone when we think of it? Is not the present the ever-moving boundary between past and future? But a moving boundary is not a place to stand upon. "If nothing were given to us except the 'no more' of the past and the 'not yet' of the future, we would not have anything" (Tillich, 1963, p. 130). The mystery is that we have a present, and in that present the past and future are ours.

Thus, when we say words such as "now" or "today," we stop the flux of time. In the same way, the beginning phrases of fairy tales halt the flow of time by calling attention to the present, and at that very moment children gain entry to a dimension of time that transcends their static representations of it. They begin to live in a present that reaches beyond the symbolic into the ineffable inner depth that gives mankind both a temporal and an "eternal now" (Tillich, 1963). In the magical realm of fairy tales children can rest in a presence through which they can forget what has passed and find courage for what is to come. Through fairy tales children are allowed to dream consciously, while the collective wisdom represented in the story gives form to the emerging fantasy and guides them toward an acceptable conclusion by envisioning a peaceful future.

As a matter of fact, just as fairy tales begin by envisioning a misty past, so do they end with allusions to a dimly lit future imbued with trust and hope. The tale "Jack the Giant Killer," for instance, is brought to a close with the following expression of faith in the future: "and there Jack and his wife lived in great contentment and happiness for many a year." Likewise, "Hansel and Gretel" ends by optimistically saying that, "Hansel and Gretel and their father never again wanted for anything," while "Snow-White" is concluded in a spirit of hope by indicating that, "Snow-White and the Prince lived long and reigned happily over their land for many, many years."[7] Thus, fairy tales lead the child back into the symbolic structure of time without sacrificing the renewed strength generated by communion with an "eternal now."

Since in each of these stories emotions are personified as princes, princesses, ghosts, monsters, witches, giants, and the like, children are able to project their own feelings onto the characters in the fairy tale. They are thereby given opportunities to give conscious expression to, and gain control over, their most primordial feelings. These feelings, if not represented and coped with in controlled fantasy, gain access to conscious expression by means of nighttime dreams as well as in other less restrained forms of fantasy such as nightmares, self-delusion, escapism, denial, and other defense mechanisms.

In general, just as discursive symbols are used to structure spatial and temporal perceptions meaningfully into a latent topology, so are nondiscursive symbols represented in dreams and fantasy used to uncover an underlying purpose in the whole of life. A significant question to be asked, therefore, is the degree to which children in American culture are learning to use the magic of fantasy to establish control of their feelings and to envision the tacit meaning hidden in their lives as opposed to being driven to despair by the specter of unknown forces distorted by a veil of defenses.

Vision of Destiny or Specter of Despair?

In that regard, call to mind the fact that in Western cosmology mankind is perceived as being suspended in, but is not viewed as being part of, a matrix of abstract time, space, and causality, i.e., the Kantian categories of mind. The universe, therefore, is envisioned

---

[7]Not all stories lead the child to resolution of conflict and an optimistic outlook on the future, however. For help in selecting tales that offer meaning instead of despair, the reader is encouraged to study Bruno Bettelheim's (1976) book entitled *The uses of enchantment*, in which he discusses the importance of fairy tales in the lives of children. Also of use in acquiring a deeper appreciation of the significance of myths and fantasy in children's feeling, valuing, and growing is Madeleine L'Engle's (1977) commentary.

as being outside rather than inside the self, so that knowledge of man's place in the scheme stems from sources outside, instead of inside, the person. Hence the inclination is not to give credence to images of life arising from the depths of humanity's inner being as portrayed in dreams and fantasy, while information obtained by looking outside the individual is regarded as being infallible. Since time and space are viewed as being exterior to life, they are seen as obstacles to overcome and as frontiers to conquer rather than as extensions of mankind's own being. These are extensions in which there exists a reality hidden from view, but in which individual and collective destinies may be fulfilled and in which callings may be heard (Kluckhohn and Strodtbeck, 1961; Polanyi, 1959, 1967).

Among the more significant consequences of this prevailing cosmology is that children in American culture typically are not encouraged to attend to or to use the inner power of fantasy in expressing their feelings, gaining control of their lives, and searching for the meaning hidden in each of their lives. Instead they are socialized to turn their fantasy against themselves by repressing and denying in conscious awareness any messages originating from the deeper recesses of their being. Despite the fact that their most elemental fears and aspirations reach conscious expression through dreams and fantasy (Jung, 1940), children are seldom taught to use their fantasy to find meaning and enrich their life. For example, in a recent study of children's fears (Bauer, 1976), I discovered that from early (kindergarten) to later (sixth grade) childhood ages, children become progressively more reluctant to admit to having fears with imaginary themes or to experiencing frightening dreams. In fact, by about age 12, only 10 per cent of boys I interviewed were willing to reveal to me that they had frightening dreams. That the resistance of the boys to tell about their dreams was rooted in the socialization process was suggested by the fact that 70 per cent of the girls indicated that dreams were a source of fear.

Paradoxically, in a desperate attempt to defend themselves against despair children seem to deny and repress their deepest fears, while they use these same mechanisms to ignore the hope that issues from the soul of mankind. Regrettably the tendency in American culture is not to guide children toward trust in *self* and

faith in their future but toward self-alienation and fear of the unknown. Rare indeed is the child who is taught to listen for the silent
messages emanating from within, as he or she consciously seeks to
find the contribution of an individual life to the collective destiny of
mankind.

In closing, from the beginning to the last syllable of time, children
are born into, live, and die in a world of symbols, and the pattern in
the development of their symbolic representations of reality (a topology) bears witness to the presence of a tacit dimension that
underlies mankind's individual and collective existence but is hidden from man's conscious awareness. Each person comes from a
"being-not-yet" (time before birth), lives in an "eternal now," and
returns to a "being-no-more" (time after death). The meaning of life
is created in the process of consciously searching for the design
under the surface while composing in the sand of time an image of a
unique soul. Just as the meaning of a symphony transcends the
notes representing single sounds and is known only at its conclusion, so too is the meaning of an individual life discovered only in
relation to other lives, transcendent of any symbolic representation
of it, and not realized until the last note is sounded. Regardless of its
timbre or its tempo, the melody played in each life makes a unique
contribution to the symphony emerging in the future of human being, so that when the final note in the history of earth echoes
through space and time, the spirit of mankind will transcend its
symbolic representations to reside in the eternal. Beyond mankind's
symbolic images of time and space is the unspeakable. Between *I*
and *Thou* is a tacit dimension known only to those who have courage enough for a personal encounter with the rich life within, with
the spirituality of the other, and with the silent reality visible
through the golden gleam of dreams and fantasy.

For those of us responsible for the lives of children, therefore, the
challenge is clear. Do we have the courage to live in the life-space of
our children, so that we can guide them toward realization of their
selves, toward recognition of the realm between man and man, and
toward sensitivity to the hidden dimension glimmering through the
magic of dreams and fantasy? In the face of a dominant world view
haunted by the specter of despair, dare we help our children envision
faith and uncover destiny in an unknown tomorrow?

DWELLING IN CHILDREN'S SPACE AND TIME

In what ways can we teachers and teachers-to-be dwell in the life-space of children, so that we may come to better understandings of their views of time and space?

Several times in this chapter I illustrated that much can be learned about the child's image of space and time by listening carefully and sensitively to verbal expressions and by examining drawings, paintings, and other creations of young children. At older age levels, personal documents generated by children in the form of written autobiographies, dramatic productions, dream content, personal diaries and journals, letters, art forms of various types, projective representations, scrap books, collections, memorabilia, and the like can be revealing as well. For the interested teacher, many of these methods along with additional ways of fathoming the child's view of his or her life-space are discussed in detail in Millie Almy's *Ways of Studying Children* (1979) and in Kaoru Yamamoto's *The Child and His Image* (1972).

Our comprehension and appreciation of the perceptions revealed in children's personal documents depend, however, on our own visions of these dimensions of life. Teachers now are invited to join us as we attempt to broaden and deepen our insight into the mystery of space and time. Care enough to journey with us as we searchingly probe into that multifarious realm in the subsequent chapters of this book, and be bold enough to follow paths marked in the annotated bibliography below. If you dare to, we shall all be made richer and, perhaps, a little wiser.

Suggested Readings

Berman, Louise, & Roderick, Jessie (Eds.). *Feeling, valuing and the art of growing: Insights into the affective.* Washington, D.C.: Association for Supervision and Curriculum Development, 1977.

In this provocative book, authors drawn from art, education, literature, psychology, natural science, and sociology offer the reader a series of truly insightful commentaries on the meaning of life in education.

Bettelheim, Bruno. *The uses of enchantment: the meaning and importance of fairy tales.* New York: Knopf, 1976.

Written by one of the twentieth century's most original child psychologists and perceptive personalities, this book reveals how fairy tales are an irreplaceable heritage for educating, supporting, and liberating the emotions of children. This work is useful to all who search for a deeper understanding of the importance of fantasy in the life of children.

Bühler, Charlotte, & Massarick, Fred (Eds.). *The course of human life.* New York: Springer, 1968.

This unique book is the product of the combined efforts of 16 authors who focus their discussion on the problem of goal setting from a humanistic perspective. Their thesis is that since goal setting leads to eventual fulfillment or failure in life, it must be understood in the context of human life as a whole. To lead a goal-directed life means to have the desire to see one's life culminating in certain results.

Cassirer, Ernst. *An essay on man.* New Haven: Yale University Press, 1944.

In this book one of this century's greatest philosophers examines mankind's efforts to understand itself and to deal with the problems of its universe through the creation and use of symbols.

Fraisse, Paul. *The psychology of time.* New York: Harper & Row, 1963.

For readers interested in a comprehensive review of literature and research bearing on the development of the conception of time from infancy to adulthood, this work is an excellent resource.

Laurendeau, Monique, & Pinard, Adrien. *The development of the concept of space in the child.* New York: International Universities Press, 1970.

This volume presents a detailed critical analysis of both the tests and concepts used by Jean Piaget in explaining the methods by which children form space concepts. Though somewhat technical in content, it is thorough in its discussion of an important aspect of the child's development.

Polanyi, Michael. *The study of man.* Chicago: University of Chicago Press, 1958.

In three readable essays—"Understanding Ourselves," "The Calling of Man," and "Understanding History"—this seminal book serves as a good introduction to Polanyi's other works and advances his comprehensive theory of human understanding.

Humankind is inescapably a creature and a creator of its world. On the shared loom of each culture, individual children weave space and time into a unique pattern of their own. The woven fabric, in turn, becomes the child. This enigmatic process of reciprocal creation is the story of the following chapter, a story of personal quest across time and space.

Trails of Many, and of One:
The Wholesome Child, the Troubled Child

KAORU YAMAMOTO

In a sense, an infant requires very little. For the newborn to take the first few major steps in the long process of humanization, it needs merely to "experience a warm, intimate, and continuous relationship" with a mothering figure or figures (Bowlby, 1965, p. 13). Continuity seems critical, and so does the quality of the caring relationship. Since the baby's attachment to the human community is still very tenuous, various elements in his or her environment have to be as constant and stable as possible.

Interruptions and upheavals in the interaction between the caregiver and receiver tend to cast a long, dark shadow over the latter's development (Goldstein, Freud, and Solnit, 1973). The child's, and not adults', sense of time prevails in this experience. As elucidated in other chapters, the younger the child, the less meaningful the physical time, and the more urgent his or her physiological and conative demands. In other words, the duration of a given experience is not to be understood in clock time, but according to the young's private feelings.

Likewise, contiguity or proximity counts. The mothering figure has to be there in flesh to personify what Sullivan (1953a) called the "good mother" and "bad mother" patterns of encounter. Out of both of these, the child gradually builds a more complex perception of people in the world. It is interesting to note that Bowlby's influential theory of attachment and separation (1969, 1973) is essentially an interpretation of the mother-child relationship in terms of physical distance between the two interactants. The critical role of close bodily contacts in the development of *Homo sapiens* has also been emphasized by Montagu (1971).

The human intimacy the young child needs has a large spatial, as well as temporal, component to it.

THE QUEST

Granted the crucial importance of the warmth, continuity, and stability of the caring relationship, the experience is not solely a matter of adult provision. As Goldstein, Freud, and Solnit (1973) cautioned:

> The problem is that some workers in the child care service have learned the lesson of environmental influence too well. Consequently they view the child as a mere adjunct to the adult world, a passive recipient of parental impact. They tend to ignore that children interact with the environment on the basis of their individual innate characteristics. . . . To see children too one-sidedly as mirroring their backgrounds blinds the observer to the uniqueness of their vital characteristics on which their own specific developmental needs are based. (pp. 10-11)

From the earliest days, infants do act to exert influence on the quality of their lives. Within their obviously narrow repertoire, and in consonance with their particular images of life, these seemingly powerless beings strive to change and control their worlds. Thus, it is as meaningful to speak of the infant's influence on the caregiver (Lewis and Rosenblum, 1974) as to discuss the dynamics in reverse. Through various modes of posture, motility, vocalization, and the like, babies not only regulate what others do to, for, or with them in the immediate, but also lay the foundation for the development of a full-fledged, autonomous self (Ainsworth and Bell, 1974) by being, and enjoy being, the cause of events. Limited as the boundaries of their kingdoms may be, and fancied or real, they are still the master!

Trailblazers All

One of the most remarkable observations on human beings, which has become increasingly well established over the past quarter century, is that each child literally creates his or her own world. The youngster recreates much of what all others have created before, but also adds some unique variations. In the mid-1940s, Montessori (1969) anticipated our current understanding by stating, "We used to say it was the mother who formed the child; for it is she who teaches him to walk, talk, and so on. But none of this is really done by the mother. It is an achievement of the child. What the mother brings forth is the baby, but it is the baby who produces the man" (p. 16).

In a small tome very appropriately titled *To understand is to invent,* Piaget (1974) summarized his work on human cognition by saying that, "to understand is to discover, or reconstruct by discovery. . ."(p. 20), and "every new truth to be learned [is to] be rediscovered or at least reconstructed by the student, and not simply imparted to him" (p. 15).

On the basis of one's unique endowment and experience, a child builds his or her own scheme of understanding and continually revises it within and across the different stages of development. No one else but the child can construct this scheme to make some sense out of a given corner of life. It is indeed miraculous that most individuals arrive at a more or less similar conception of the world and, needless to say, that would be impossible without the communal existence of humans and the resultant world of culture (Sullivan, 1953b).

A similar picture of creativity on the part of the child has also been revealed in recent studies in the realm of language. With the initial impetus coming mainly from Chomsky and his colleagues in the late 1950s, these analyses have strongly suggested that children in fact *develop* their own languages, rather than learn an adult language in a piecemeal fashion (Brown, 1973; Cazden, 1972). Granted that models of mature language behaviors must be there, children do not imitate them for direct internalization. Instead they infer a small number of basic rules from these examples and, out of this implicitly constructed rule system, generate and transform an almost infinite variety of acceptable sentences (most of which they have never heard from anyone else). This active, nonimitative process of construction is shown in such pronouncements of alleged infantile mistakes as, "He did it hisself," or "I goed there." The basic rules underlying these constructions are actually correct, even though the irregularities in adult language itself make the statements appear to be in error.

Another instance of the construction process in the child may be seen by examining the formation of [race] attitudes. Goodman (1964) had this to say about the dynamics involved:

> To call this process a matter of "transmission" is to imply a misleading simplicity, directness, and mechanical handing-over (or teaching). The process is perhaps less a matter of *transmission* than of *regeneration*. This is to say that there begins early and proceeds gradually, in each individual, a process much more complex than the sheer *learning* of someone else's attitudes. It is rather that each individual *generates* his own attitudes, out of the personal, social, and cultural materials which happen to be his. (p. 246)

What a child reveals in the construction of cognition, language, and attitudes is but an example of a more inclusive process of human adaptation, a process aimed at an increase of autonomy. Making sense out of life, taking control of one's world, and enhancing the extent of self-determination, all derive from the postulated fundamental tendency of *Homo sapiens* to seek self-actualization (Goldstein, 1939), to become instead of just to be (Allport, 1955), to aim at fully-functioning self (Rogers, 1961), and to be growth motivated (Maslow, 1968).

The course of general development reflects this quest for autonomy in a movement away from the iron grip of the here-and-now concerns to the less immediate and less egocentric. The marked intolerance for postponement of gratification of wishes and impulses decreases, and the capacity to withstand and accept one's frustration and anxiety increases. The child comes to be able to build and maintain close emotional ties with many different people across space and time and to expand the horizon of his or her perspective by reaching out into both the past (memory) and the future (hope). This broadening of the vista will encompass a deeper and deeper look into one's self, as well as into the souls of others, so that the child finally comes to realize for whom the bell tolls.

An Opening Vista

The central process of human adaptation may be more closely examined in terms of three clusters of strategies: those of mastery, coping, and defense (White, 1960, 1976). From the very beginning, infants are known to exhibit a notable inclination for exploring themselves and their environment, even when their physiological needs have been well satisfied. Babies continue to work on various facets of their world to master life tasks of increasing cognitive and manipulative complexity. This leads to both adaptive skills and a sense of competence.

Two familiar acts of children epitomize the strategies of mastery. As tersely noted by Berg (1972), "Fantasy is an exploration of living reality, and play a rehearsal of living reality, and we use them both as tools of growth that will help us first understand our reality, and then help us shape it with awareness and competence" (p. 120).

The paradoxes of play are numerous. One is that this essentially autotelic (an end in itself) activity in fact shows much directedness, selectivity, and persistence. These characteristics of purposive action betray a scheme of understanding already elaborated or in the offing, which underlies even the "seemingly most disorganized behavior" of the child (Piaget, 1963, p. 401). If it is to add to the child's exploration, integration, and transcendence, play must nevertheless stay in its unique autotelic sphere under his or her control. Little regard is to be given such matters as the tangible results, productivity, or efficiency, and the whole sphere must be free of the familiar time-space constraints of heterotelic (means to other ends) activity. No doubt the elements of gaming with all its social implications will enter the scene sooner or later; still, play has to remain as free of exigencies of actuality as possible, if it is to allow children "to deal with experience by creating model situations and to master reality by experiment and planning" (Erikson, 1963, p. 222).

The young, and the old as well for that matter, must be able to engage in such reformulation of their experience so that they may relive it, digest it, and incorporate it into their reconstructed and expanded schemes of understanding without much intervention or anxiety. In play, so protected, life can be stopped and resumed at will. Time can be readily compressed and expanded in the play sphere, and the child can be an inhabitant simultaneously of an endless variety of lands near and far, old and new, likely and unlikely. Thus, play is one of the most potent means at children's disposal for attaining mastery over themselves and their worlds.

A large part of the constructive function of play derives from the encouragement that fantasy provides the child. It is easy for adults to forget how overwhelmingly frightening, devastatingly disappointing, and crushingly frustrating life can be, and is, for young children. As their bliss appears to see no ceiling, so their despair seems to know no floor. Life being what it is, they are destined to face many a defeat while steadily moving towards autonomy by taking on one new challenge after another.

> Considerable as the child's real achievements are, they seem to vanish into insignificance when compared to his failures, if only because he has no comprehension of what is actually possible. This disillusionment may lead to such severe disappointment in himself that the child may give up all effort and completely withdraw into himself, away from the world, unless fantasy comes to his rescue. (Bettelheim, 1976, pp. 124-5)

Fantasy comes to the rescue by reestablishing the child as an amphibian (Huxley, 1962) in the here-and-now *and* there-and-then. It expands the time perspective to place the present difficulties against future possibilities. It broadens the realm of experience to integrate the real with make-believe, the concrete with abstract, and the known with visionary. It reaffirms the child as the prime agent and actor instead of a helpless pawn under the control of capricious and sinister alien forces, either internal or external. To these assertive ends, various art forms offer inestimable assistance

(Bettelheim, 1976; Chukovsky, 1963; Read, 1957; Way, 1967). Be they largely performative in nature (dance, music, drama), productive (painting, sculpture, poetry), or interpretive (dreams, fairy tales), a careful study of their creative functions in childhood would definitely be beneficial.

The Pace Quickens

When a fairly drastic change confronts the child or when his or her familiar ways of handling life's vagaries are found wanting, novel means of adaptation are called for. Such endeavors to manage rather trying conditions are subsumed under the strategies of coping. More than in most mastery situations, uncomfortable affects like anxiety, guilt, shame, or grief are in evidence to place an added burden on the child. The basic patterns of these coping strategies appear to be established early to withstand the test of time through stressful developmental transitions (Murphy and Moriarty, 1976).

With adults, recent studies by Holmes, Rahe, and their associates have indicated that many family-related events like marriage, divorce, pregnancy, and childbirth are indeed regarded across different cultures (e.g., United States, Scandinavia, Europe, and Japan) as crises that tax one's capacity to cope. Together with other changes in employment status, health, residential location, and the like, these experiences may interact to bring the strain to a breaking point for a person.

One of the prevalent contexts of stress for children is the passage from one social institution to another; for instance, moving out of the secure circle of the family to the novel territory of the school and all that goes with it. Kindergarten, or first-grade, entry marks a major crisis for most youngsters and a disaster for some who have not been well prepared for what they are likely to encounter in the unfamiliar environment. Temporary behavioral disturbances such as tears, tantrums, thumb-sucking, vomiting, and bed-wetting are common in the initial phases of transition. Extreme school phobia may be restricted to the dyads of mutually overdependent mothers and children. However, the separation is understandably difficult not only for many youngsters but also for numerous parents who are inclined to have feelings of loss, uncertainty about their performance as parent, and fear of rivalry and estrangement. Similar periods of stress are likely to be observed at the shift from elementary school to junior high school, and again at the child's movement into high school. Given the fact that these experiences can be as stressful to parents as to children, it is obvious that the teacher's role is critical in aiding both parties in such transitions.

Another everyday example of the stress of change is found in adolescence. At least in American culture, this period of development is characterized by unsettling in-betweenness that severely tries the young. However, chances are that adolescents are dynamic, restless, volatile, idealistic, impressionable, passionate, extreme, or righteous *not because* they are young, but rather *because* of the swift and radical shifts demanded of them. "When people of whatever age group and condition are subjected to drastic change," they reveal the same kind of frantic, vascillating, and perpetual motion in search of a new birth and a new identity. "Even the old when they undergo the abrupt change of retirement may display juvenile impulses, inclinations, and attitudes" (Hoffer, 1969, p. 13). The strain of being uprooted from an established mode of life and being thrust into a new, vaguely defined and poorly modeled pattern is felt by anyone and everyone.

Individuals certainly vary in their particular ways of coping, both in the specific tactics of handling threatening tasks and in the overall strategies involving the configuration of these tactics. They may attempt to reduce the tension, bypass or postpone the challenge, set limits on or transform the situation, mount an all-out attack on the obstacle, balance the threat with an added measure of security, and so on (Murphy and associates, 1962). It has nevertheless been observed that two categories of knowledge commonly help keep a stressful experience manageable. One is the foreknowledge, or some believable warning of the imminent crisis, that allows preparatory mobilization of the person. The other is an understanding of what is taking place to permit an overall grasp of the experience. Both these serve to reduce shock and its negative aftereffects (Tanner, 1976).

Unfortunately, neither kind of knowledge would reach an individual already in an incessant, frenzied movement with closed eyes and ears, so to speak. The irony here is that while a person feels hard pressed to create a new identity apace, it actually "takes leisure to mature. People in a hurry can neither grow nor decay; they are preserved in a state of perpetual puerility" (Hoffer, 1969, p. 16). For them, the more things change, the more things remain the same! The challenge for adolescents, as well as others faced with the stress of drastic change, is for them to retain sufficient faith in themselves and in the grand scheme of this universe to be able to walk, figuratively speaking, amidst the madly dashing crowd.

The undesirability of rushing through an experience is clearly seen in coping with the generally most stressful life event of all, the demise of someone dear to us. Death casts a long shadow, and none of the three-fold tasks of the survivor (facing the immediate impact of loss, grief work, and reconstruction) can be hastily handled without further aggravation. When, for example, a child's parent dies, he or she is under enough strain not to be bothered with the unresolved difficulties among adults. Unfortunately, whether parents, teachers, and other so-called "grown-ups" are generally mature enough to be of any assistance to the young seems debatable.

> It is a paradox that the very person who is deeply afflicted himself, namely the surviving parent, is, from the child's point of view, best suited to help him grasp and handle the tragic event. When the surviving parent can sensitively fulfill this task during the difficult period of the other parent's terminal illness or at the time of his sudden death, his long-standing relationship with his child serves as a support and makes the realities more bearable for the child. (Furman, 1974, p. 17)

The task for adults is clear. Meanwhile, every new challenge that is squarely faced and satisfactorily dealt with adds to the child's adaptive skills and feeling of adequacy. Each such experience of capability ("I can") deepens the awareness of self ("I am") and builds the sense of self-worth. "Through his coping experiences the child discovers and measures himself, and develops his own perception of who and what he is and in time may become. We can say that the child creates his identity through his efforts in coming to terms with the environment in his own personal way" (Murphy and associates, 1962, p. 374).

THE DARK OF THE FOREST

Tanner (1976) observed that the Chinese word for crisis expresses something that is missing in its English counterpart. Theirs consists of two characters, "one representing danger, the other representing opportunity."[1] A strange fact about crisis is that, "while it can be a brush with disaster, a potential loss, it can also be a chance for gain; oddly, it is often both things at the same time" (p. 81).

It is indeed a tribute to the indomitable human spirit that most crises are competently coped with to bring people closer to self-determination. Even in such extreme contexts as Nazi concentration camps, where one's fate was totally under the captors' whimsical control and one's life utterly uncertain and ignominious, the basic quest for autonomy went on with amazing ingenuity and resiliency, if not in action or creation, then at least in attitude (Frankl, 1969). Still, if danger and anxiety continue to mount and persist, adaptation becomes increasingly more difficult, even with the deployment of all the defense mechanisms at one's disposal, e.g., repression, projection, reaction formation, and regression. Under these conditions, a person may finally come to the last stage in the so-called general adaptation syndrome. In Selye's model (1956), this stage of exhaustion and collapse follows those of, respectively, alarm (alert and mobilization) and resistance (adaptive efforts).

Straying Paths

One of the most pathetic casualties of overwhelming stress is the child whose desperate, yet futile, attempts under very difficult circumstances have brought forth a pattern of behavior generally identified as infantile autism.[2] In such a child, we witness an instance of

---

[1] In point of fact, this is incorrect. The second character actually stands for "moment," and the word "crisis" equals "a moment of danger." The same character appears in another two-character word, "opportunity," which is "a potential or propitious moment." This misinterpretation nevertheless makes a good point about crisis experiences and, for that reason, I am letting it stand here.

[2] Autism is not the only form of serious schizophrenic disorder in childhood. However, its indications become apparent much earlier than others, frequently during the second year of life. In contrast, "It is usual to reserve the term *childhood schizophrenia* for disorders that make their appearance after the first four or five years" (White, 1964, p. 532). In the latter, a very strong symbiotic pattern is common between mother and child, thus strangling each other against independence. The situation reminds one of that noted in school phobia. For more technical discussion of autism, see sources like Bettelheim (1967), Lovaas (1976), Ritvo (1976), and Wing (1976).

the most tragic human efforts at making sense and taking control of one's own world. Here, we see how crucial self-determination is for an individual to grow fully human.

> The human experience is built up on our sense of space, time, and causality.... What made us what we are was not simply that we recognized causal relations, but what followed from it: the conviction that a sequence of events can be changed through our influence.... It is when we feel we cannot influence the most important things that happen to us, when they seem to follow the dictates of some inexorable power, that we give up trying to learn how to act on, or change them. (Bettelheim, 1967, p. 51)

And the child gives up, but not without a struggle. First, he or she may have to let go of time, since "where there is no hope . . . time loses significance" (Henry, 1973, p. 12). The child's actions do not lead to any difference-making occurrences, and no predictions carry any meaning except the forecast that nothing follows one's action. "But if nothing happens, there is no life. And this is exactly the conviction of these children: that they have no life because they cannot give it any direction" (Bettelheim, 1967, p. 54). Elsewhere, similar sentiments were expressed by a schizophrenic patient to Searles (1960) in the following exchange: "[the woman] asked with a bereft facial expression and in an anxious tone as she sat down next to me, 'Do you think there is any world there?' I replied, warmly and reassuringly, 'Sure—there's plenty of world there. You doubt it sometimes?' To this she said, in a way which left me deeply moved, 'I doubt there is any world left, because of my experiences.'" (p. 167).

With time thus rendered peculiarly meaningless,[3] space is left alone. This space the child must now arrange in such a way as to insure the maximum possible security. If things are rigidly ordered and placed to insure the sameness, not however in terms of the permanence or constancy of objects as such, but in terms of their

---

[3]Some variations in the pattern of concerns with, or structuring of, time have been reported in relation to several diagnostic categories (e.g., Farnham-Diggory, 1966; Matarrazo, 1962; Yaker, Osmond, and Cheek, 1972). Granted that such "deviations" (Doob, 1971) are an integral part of these peoples' current adaptive styles, the developmental history of the differences remains little known. The role played by the classification, labeling, and treatment experiences per se is also largely unknown.

positions, the status quo will be preserved. No change, thus no catastrophe and no disappointment. To see any new elements introduced into this static world would be disastrous. Repetitive, mechanical, and ritualistic treatment of separate objects, including one's own body parts and other people, makes them stand still, pigeonholed, manageable on a one-at-a-time basis, and safe.

When a child does not act upon the world, there is little chance for him or her to move out of the basic egocentric stance. Renunciation of interaction means an arrest of much of the cognitive processes at the sensorimotor level prior to the development of fully representational functions, thus severely restricting both thought and language. More seriously, the gestalt of the child's self remains diffuse in the absence of the "looking-glass" relations so crucial for the clarification of one's self-concept. Lacking recourse to the balancing and calibrating means of validation through others' eyes, a clear sense of identity (the feelings of "This is *me*" and "It is *I* that sees me, relates to you, and causes things to happen") is hard to come by.

Under these circumstances, it would be extremely difficult for the child to go beyond the munication or soliloquy stage to reach the domain of communication or human interaction. Indeed, such children may not even be able to play because of the inability to step momentarily outside of themselves so that they may entertain some "as if" possibilities without being promptly overwhelmed by immense anxiety, compelling an immediate acting out instead of play action, fantasy, or play acting (Ekstein, 1966). It is probably no accident that some of these deeply troubled children equate themselves with, or feel in the iron grip of, a machine, which is inanimate, reiterative, powerful, yet predictable.

The Waylayers

Controversies over the precise etiology of infantile autism or, for that matter, most other forms of adaptive disturbance continue to rage. There is no point in becoming embroiled in any simplistic nature-nurture argument. In any case, from where the child stands, there is no denying that the affective configuration of the family into which he or she happens to be born makes quite a bit of difference in the manner of one's movement along the pathway to autonomy. After all, "nothing in human life . . . is secured in its origin unless it is verified in the intimate meeting of partners in favorable social settings" (Erikson, 1964, p. 116).

In this light, Bettelheim (1976) recounts a revealing story about a child who finally emerged out of her total autistic withdrawal after a prolonged therapy. Reflecting upon what characterized good parent to her, "she said: 'They hope for you.' The implication was that her parents had been bad parents because they had failed both to feel hope for her and to give her hope for herself and her future life in this world" (p. 125). Hopelessness kills. It is no exaggeration to say that, while a person can survive nearly a month without food, about a week without water, and a few minutes without air, one cannot survive at all, at least as a human being, the total absence of love, hope, and faith.

Hope does not spring in a vacuum, and hopeless adults cannot hope for, and with, their children. For its beginnings, hope relies on the infant's experiencing a warm, trustworthy, and calm parenting. To provide such care, in turn, parents need to be secure in hope based upon both individual and collective experiences that affirm and support this endeavor in an integrating perspective over the past, present, and future. Thus, individuals who have never been at ease with themselves, never enjoyed a mutually satisfying relationship with others, never felt the richness of communal resources, and never come to terms with humankind as a carrier of life would indeed be ill-equipped to provide a conducive environment for the development of a hopeful child. Reciprocally, a hopeless child is not likely to inspire hope in parents, and the vicious circle unfortunately closes.

In his close study of several families with at least one psychotic child, Henry (1963, 1973) observed many exaggerated instances of a home milieu that offers little joy, compassion, or a generally positive orientation to life. Humiliation and exploitation of vulnerability abound, and family members are withdrawn from and distrustful of each other. Parental ambivalence is betrayed in their conflicting, yet simultaneous messages sent over different channels (manifest contents vs. affective tone, verbal vs. action), their treatment of children as if they were nonexistent, objects, adults, or enemies, their physical or psychological unavailability when most needed, and other similar behaviors. Parents' misconceptions about self include a confusion on time—they tend to live "as a hope that which should be a memory, and . . . as a memory what should be a hope" (Henry, 1973, p. 200). Little initiative is shown in the face of open opportunities since, in their confounded world, these possibilities have already vanished in the past. When, on the other hand, it is wise to come to terms with what has passed, they would rather continue to believe in an illusory future as if nothing had transpired.

In the web of tangled daily interactions, children continue to act, even though their adaptive actions may weave abnormal patterns in extreme cases.[4] The total configuration of family dynamics must be errant over a sustained period of time before it finally shreds the resilient fabric of the child.

> *One form of abuse alone does not make a child mad* [saving, of course, that most destructive of all abuses, isolation]. *It is an accumulation of miseries, backed up always by disorientation in the parents.* An abused child will become emotionally ill, but he will not be psychotic unless his parents are disoriented—adrift in time, unable to tell actor from acted on, easily thrown off by new situations, never sure that they mean what they say, mixed up in speech, forgetful, etc. Nor will a mixed up or even psychotic parent produce an insane child if the child is loved—if he is permitted to be a child and not a garbage pail or a phantom. He may be mixed up, but he will not be mad. (Henry, 1963, p. 387; his italics)

To Catch a Breath

No matter how bizarre and senseless it may appear to outsiders, a given pattern of adaptive behaviors becomes more intelligible when held against a backdrop of the particular social matrix. In a highly disruptive family context, a child is, and is made to feel, at the mercy of others. The valiant struggle for self-determination is made

---

[4]Alas, the extremes may not be that rare! As of July 1967, the United States Census Bureau reported that there were more than 93 million young people under age 25, two-thirds of whom were under 14. Of these children and youth, it has been estimated that 10-12 percent (more than 10 million) have major emotional difficulties to require knowledgeable professional help. Up to 3 per cent, or 3 million, are severely disturbed with a psychosis or prepsychotic condition. Unfortunately, moreover, only about ½ million youngsters are currently being served by mental health professionals (Joint Commission on Mental Health of Children, 1970).

against heavy odds and may eventually lead to a thorough conviction of nonbeing, of total worthlessness, and of hopelessness. "The absence of self-respect is a central issue in all functional disturbances. The most important task of therapy is not to have the patient gain insight into his unconscious, but to restore him to a high degree of justified self-esteem" (Bettelheim, 1975, pp. 21-22).

Overcoming the child's feelings of utter insignificance is obviously a long and difficult process that has to be sustained by others' "full human presence" (May, 1967, p. 81). However, as Bettelheim (1975) succinctly put it, "Neither freedom, nor autonomy, nor self-esteem, nor a positive outlook on life or oneself, nor friendship, not to mention love, can be forced on a person" (p. 64). That is the reason why it is critical for the whole helping milieu to convey a consistent message of love, hope, and faith, to which the child may, in time, opt to respond.

Much of this communication is done nonverbally and, typically, unawares. "It is amazing how sensitive even otherwise defensive children are to the 'atmosphere' which the very location, the architectural design, the space distribution of the house, the arrangement and type of furnishings, the equipment, the style of housekeeping suggest" (Redl and Wineman, 1957, p. 284). Some buildings suggest themselves to be a prison for life confinement, while others invite children in for rest and recuperation needed for future action. Some rooms are designed and furnished to maximize economy and managerial efficiency at whatever human cost,[5] while others show that these children are of great importance to us, if not yet to themselves. The diffuse sense of self in the autistic child, and other psychotics, and the blurred boundaries between the animate and inanimate spheres make the nonhuman environment all the more significant (Searles, 1960).

In the same vein, confusion between the symbol and symbolized, the whole and parts, or the code and contents leads to a very rigid, literal interpretation of every item, every act. Something *categorically is,* instead of contextually represents or stands for. To a par-

---

[5]This orientation was poignantly depicted in the remarks of a first grader, recorded by Uslander, Weiss, Telman, and Wernick (1974, p. 99): "I don't like to bring my friends home because we have to play outside.... Some people care more about furniture than they care about children."

ticular child, the color of red *is* poison—no "maybes" about it, no "depends." Fire *is* evil; wind *is* good. Apples are mother's milk, and so are balloons; but real milk is not milk! Needless to say, food is fraught with such absolute interpretations, and the activities of eating and elimination are often the arena for most vicious battles within the family and most critical moves within therapy.

"For psychotics of all ages, every experience becomes a symbol of intention and attitude, which matters far more to them than the experience's rational purpose and meaning. . . . Everything has its private meanings and secret messages. . . . If we want to reach the psychotic, we must resort to the symbol first of all, long before we can count on reaching him through rational thought" (Bettelheim, 1975, pp. 126-127). The same applies to words as a special class of symbols. Meanings carried by a given word tend to be highly private rather than public, i.e., shared, and concrete rather than abstract, to make verbalizations little understandable to others. The personal code is nevertheless there to be deciphered, and initial contacts of therapeutic nature must be in the child's peculiar language, not in the social one of adults (Parker, 1971; Sechehaye, 1951). In the translation work, such nonverbal media as doll play, dance, music, and art may be invaluable in aiding the tenuous communication (e.g., Alvin, 1975; Ekstein, 1966; Naumburg, 1973; Schoop, 1974).

THE DAWN TO COME

Even under conditions generally benign for development, the road to autonomy is an arduous, winding one. For anyone whose hope has been shattered from the very outset, the journey will be immensely more difficult and slow-moving. Such a child has to go a long way before he or she can feel, "Here *I* am," not anymore as a worthless object among all the other rubble, but as a worthwhile individual with a clear sense of self in a unique life-space that is liberally inhabited by other self-respecting and caring people. The child has to travel far before he or she can incorporate the fruits of past experiences to enrich the present, chart her or his course in relation to the image of self-in-the-future, and ultimately transcend the physical frame of existence to live by meaning (Frankl, 1963; May 1973).

Significantly, while the distance varies with different runners, the race set before them is shared by all. Growth is gradual, typically painstakingly so. "Time moves on. Changes come into being slowly—almost imperceptibly. Like the shift of seasons. Barely noticeable, the changing, till the change is there" (Baruch, 1964, p. 227; tense changed).

None can live and grow without love, hope, and faith. From the depth of their despair, these children in distress remind us of this. "If out of a desire to help them, we penetrate the darkness of their souls, we cannot help shedding light into the hidden recesses of our own minds" (Bettelheim, 1975, p. 589). Therefore, let us all persevere, for their sake and for ours.

Suggested Readings

For a closer look at the world of deeply troubled children and the desirable milieu for working with them, the following two books are informative:

Bettelheim, Bruno. *The empty fortress.* New York: Free Press, 1967.
Bettleheim, Bruno. *A home for the heart.* New York: Bantam Books, 1975.

Detailed descriptions of the tangled web of family relationships with which such children are likely to have to contend are given in sources such as:

Henry, Jules. *Culture against man.* New York: Vintage, 1963.
Henry, Jules. *Pathways to madness.* New York: Vintage, 1973.

The long, but fortunately successful, struggle for self-determination by some of these children is touchingly told in such records as:

Axline, Virginia M. *Dibs in search of self.* New York: Ballantine, 1964.
Baruch, Dorothy W. *One little boy.* New York: Dell, 1964.
D'Ambrosio, Richard. *No language but a cry.* New York: Dell, 1970.

*The following discussion was derived from the plenary
sessions at the Austin, Texas, retreat, October 22-24,
1976. Most of the specific comments and suggestions
offered in these discussion meetings have since been
incorporated into the revised chapters. However, some
remaining observations of general interest seemed to
justify a separate chapter. The materials were edited,
where appropriate, specific references added, and the
overall tone was left conversational.*

Children in Time and Space:
Discussion

KAORU YAMAMOTO, EDITOR

K.E.Y.: I must confess that after initiating this project and getting
you all to agree to write chapters or read them, I have been
finding it rather impossible even to talk sensibly about
this whole issue of time and space. These two dimensions of
life so thoroughly permeate everything we do, it is totally,
utterly impossible for me to grasp the scope of what I step-
ped into!

L.M.B.: That was my feeling, also.

G.M.H.: I think that's an important message, though. The thing
that struck me was the realization that teachers commonly
think of teaching about time and space by saying, "Here
are the simple one, two and threes." It is not that at all.

J.E.B.: Merely to think about time and space boggles your mind, and you cannot really think. . . .

K.E.Y.: Whatever one comes to perceive, any particular way of understanding, is only part of the elephant.

G.M.H.: Right, and the other thing is that teachers are no different from anyone else in a given culture. Teachers deal with time and space in the same way all others do—having difficulty even in becoming conscious of how they do deal with them. But, they are put in a position of having to try and teach something about the unseen elephant to children.

C.L.W.: I guess there is a realistic reason why this sort of book has seldom been written before!

PERVASIVE, YET ELUSIVE

H.D.D.: The point on the cultural frame of reference seems important, but even that is not simple—not monolithic. For instance, when we mention Western civilization, we behave as if it were a single civilization, large, urban-oriented, technological, and so on. All these things sort of flow into the phrase, but there is much of Western civilization that is not like that. Let us not overgeneralize.

D.H.B.: You are right, and there are some Eastern civilizations that are highly technological. . . .

H.D.D.: Yes. For instance, here in the United States we stress the value of promptness more than anywhere else in the West except perhaps in Switzerland and Germany. Yet, I think nothing is as prompt and time-oriented anywhere in the world as the Japanese railroad train! It starts on time and arrives on time. You can call that Western civilization if you wish, transplanted Western civilization, maybe. It is certainly an application of the whole technological miracle to urban living.

O.L.D.: I want to say something here. In the history of ideas, the history of technology, the pocket watch is very important because you could never insist that someone be on time until he or she carried a practical chronometer. Unless someone has a watch available, a person is not going to be able to be on time. [According to Priestly (1968), pocket watches have been made since the mid-seventeenth century, but these delicate instruments were not in common use until nearly a century later.] "On time" in Jefferson's day was tea time that could cover two or three hours. It is promptness, alright, but a different kind. Now, at least in the United States, this notion of punctuality or timeliness is not just a function of the pocket watch. The promptness, which we understand particularly in schools, is a feature of the industrial revolution, symbolized in the railroad and the clocks in the factories. In other words, it is only recently that this portion of Western civilization has been concerned with that kind of thing.

K.E.Y.: Right. Historical changes indeed affect the timing of life events by providing the institutional conditions for or against these events. For example, it would have been impossible to enforce the societal requirements for school attendance, if public schools had not been readily available to accommodate children of the specified ages.

S.D.C.: That is also true of the spatial prerequisite of life experiences. I remember all the talk about the 1976 Montreal Olympics being the last of its kind, because it is becoming increasingly difficult to gather a huge number of athletes in a single city, single stadium, at a single time to celebrate human togetherness.

L.L.D.: The "double session" practice (or controversy) in many of our schools is another case in point.

C.E.M.: Before we stray further from the monolithic interpretation of Western civilization, let me say that we tend to substitute the word "western" for "technological." There is a certain world view accompanying this technological orientation, which is becoming sort of worldwide, and there are fewer and fewer cultures that have different world views or that can live within those different world views.

L.M.B.: That's a good point.

H.F.D.: Along the line somewhere we lost our crafts and the importance of doing things slowly and doing things very well, didn't we? The mercantile system and money became so important. . . .

O.L.D.: I really don't think that that was lost until the 1870s in Western Europe and the United States. Historically I think we can find evidence supporting the notion that handcraft and piecework were a function of just this pre-industrial, pre-machine, pre-mass production period.

C.E.M.: You know, to a certain extent some of the very best, Michelangelo, for example, were under a great deal of pressure. He painted the Sistine Chapel in the old style, instead of using the "modern" craftsman techniques of his day. They may not have been what we tend to view as mass production today in terms of production lines, but there was a movement toward doing things much more quickly, perhaps not as quickly as we do them now, but still very quickly, often with the help of their apprentices.

L.L.D.: On the other hand, I am not sure whether our image of handcrafted products is necessarily accurate when it comes to their precision, their quality, their benefits, or even the pleasure with which they were produced.

N.J.G.: I agree. No question about the fact that we've accepted mass production, but the presumed change in the quality of the product—that's another thing. Not everything that was produced by the old methods was of good quality.

C.E.M.: Yes, one example may be found in Sweden. The Swedes were going back to their old, traditional ways of doing things and teaching them in school. I remember my son coming home and making a candelabra out of brass. It was crooked and yet, you know, that was supposed to be *the* way to make the thing. This way of doing things took a long time and much effort. It depends on what you value.

L.M.B.: Right. I remember Riesman (1961) saying something apt about people's flight into craftsmanship hobbies as a rather futile protest against consumerism in work and play.

C.L.W.: The person who creates something has a lot to do with it. Sometimes we get much more pride out of something we make by hand, something that we create ourselves. It is of much more value than things manufactured in a mass production factory. And it will last—I mean, we tend to save those things as we save roses and press them in books.

S.D.C.: Beautiful things you have made you keep, but others you get rid of quickly—like some of the sweaters I have knit!

C.E.M.: But beauty also depends on time. Its criteria change. Many objects of art we admire today weren't beautiful in their time. The artists were not successful then. Often they had to wait until they were dead before being recognized. So, this is all relative in time.

D.H.B.: Back to the technological for a moment. I believe that in our culture now there is a tremendous emphasis on "instant time." You know, we don't want to see a ball game after it's over, we want to see it while it is going on right now. When we moved more slowly, we used to get into and out of time, so to speak. Now we are in a different relationship with time.

L.L.D.: Would another example be that Bell Telephone commercial on TV? You can be with your sister in California just by dialing. She is just a fingertip away.

J.M.B.: And the reference to the past. The past you shared with her is here and now. Friendship is forever.

C.L.W.: Really, it would take longer for you to be with or talk to your folks if they lived in the same town!

O.L.D.: That "instant time" sort of thing also involves space. My parents continually find it difficult to understand how I have time to get (fly) from, say, Dallas to New York or Los Angeles, do a job there, and get back to do my work here. My grandfather, in turn, had difficulty in comprehending the range of my father who taught in different parts of the state. My grandfather had never lived out of the county, you know.

L.M.B.: There is the matter of a changing rate of technological impact. It's an accelerating rate, and I don't think we fully appreciate the newness to our preceding generations of the technological change. Of course, we can apply the same relationship to the following generations. We are somewhat used to such a change, but our children are very much used to it.

H.D.D.: I wonder what we are paying for all that. For instance, many children nowadays do not live close to their grandparents. They may talk over the phone or visit occasionally, but they don't have the time and proximity to hear the stories of the family, not only from their grandparents but also from uncles, aunts, and so on.

K.E.Y.: Acceleration of rootlessness, truncation of heritage, or something like that, right?

H.D.D.: Right, and I feel that it is a sign of our times to see the birth of Alex Haley's *Roots* (1976), plus all the genealogical interest of lesser significance. A vague awareness of something missing, the lost legacy, if you will.

L.L.D.: Also, all this nostalgia in music, film, fashion and so on—a sort of going back and ruminating. Perhaps we have been moving so rapidly through time and space that people are starting to say, "Hey, wait a minute, I can't go this fast."

N.J.G.: A time and space to pause and look around?

L.L.D.: Ah-ha, to assimilate some of the experiences that have happened.

H.F.D.: Yes, lots of things are still unreal to me. Human beings walking on the moon, for instance. I watched that on TV, but I also saw *Flash Gordon* on it, too. Are both real? Both may be unreal.

J.E.B.: A tremendous compression of the world. People like Toffler (1970) and McLuhan (1972) have touched upon some of this.

L.M.B.: For better or worse, in our culture right now, we may be taking the present, that thin slice of existing time and space, and concentrating our efforts on making it better.

C.E.M.: That "better" can be terribly narrow though. Because we don't understand much about the past and are sort of frightened of the future, we may be retrenching ourselves in the present, trying to make the foxhole as pleasant as possible!

K.E.Y.: Ultimately the so-called "present-time" orientation is a cry of despair. Often mistakenly believed to be intrinsic in poor people, this orientation is actually rooted in uncertainty, skepticism, and pessimism about anyone's future. In that sense, it reflects a particular future-time orientation. The person has a pretty good idea of the future and its hopelessness.

D.H.B.: That's good. There must be a purpose over and beyond the immediate creature-comfort now. There must be a transcending meaning to life.

K.E.Y.: To me, there is an underlying purpose to this whole thing. A long, long-range one, extending from the past to the future of humankind.

D.H.B.: Right. There is no presence in the present without the dimension of the eternal. Tillich (1963) said that:

> Whenever we say "now" or "today," we stop the flux of time for us. We accept the present and do not care that it is gone in the moment that we accept it. We live in it, and it is renewed for us in every new "present." This is possible because every moment of time reaches into the eternal. It is the eternal that stops

> the flux of time for us. It is the eternal "now" which
> provides for us a temporal "now." (pp. 130-131)

M.M.M.: That's powerful! That's the mystery of the whole thing.

N.J.G.: The development of children's understanding of time and
space is in itself a process of unraveling the mystery, of
discovering something that is hidden all around them.
They sort of structure the world of time and space out of
their experience.

S.D.C.: And that experience includes all we parents convey to
children from the moment of birth, or even of conception.
How we handle nurturing needs, dependency needs, other
tendencies, and relationships. These needs may be similar
across cultures, but the way they are handled would be
very different from one culture to another—varied feeding
schedules, and so on. From the very outset, you present
your spatial and temporal structures and views to the
newborn through every motion and action of yours.

C.L.W.: Every child is going to see time and space differently in
that sense.

MOLDING AND BEING MOLDED

S.D.C.: As a result, it is very difficult for us to think of time and
space, or anything else for that matter, outside of our own
cultural experiences. We have to remember that constantly. Our perspectives are ours—they are not the only
ones possible or even necessarily desirable.

L.M.B.: In other words, our perspectives are space- and time-
bound. "Every epoch tends to freeze its own unique experience into an ahistorical vision of life-in-general" (Keniston, 1976, p. 192).

K.E.Y.: That awareness of relativity is critical, I believe. Plus, a
sufficient exposure to alternative perspectives and interpretations. Then, and only then, can the child finally
make a considered choice.

D.H.B.: Right, the child has to be able to make choices and take responsibilities for those choices. After all, the child is the only one who can put his or her unique meaning to life.

L.M.B.: A process of continuous purposing, so to speak.

D.H.B.: One makes a difference where one did not before. The person creates meaning . . . à la Frankl (1969), you know.

N.J.G.: Yes, we create time and space conceptions, but let's not overlook the other side of the coin. These creations of ours create us—after creating our monster, we become bound by it.

C.L.W.: We *tend* to become bound by it. We don't have to.

N.J.G.: O.K., the human mind conceives time and space. In turn, these concepts *tend* to fashion the mind.

K.E.Y.: That applies to every dimension of culture, or what Hall (1959) calls the "map of culture." Not only to time and space, but also to communication, work, sex, and so on and so forth.

H.F.D.: To make sense out of this uncertain life, we develop many strands of cosmology, and then these are inclined to shape our thoughts and feelings, is that it?

S.D.C.: This certainly applies to language, doesn't it?

C.E.M.: Yes. We tend to make the mistake of saying that other people don't know what something means, when it is simply that their concepts do not coincide with ours, or we don't know how to find out whether or not they know!

H.F.D.: A good point. An example may be to say that the Hopi have no sense of the past or the future, because their language does not have these tenses. Trying to judge everything in terms of our, or *the,* frame of reference is a sure sign of ethnocentrism. True, the Hopi do not divide the world in a rectilinear continuum, running from our "past" to "present" to "future." They have the "manifest" and "nonmanifest," and the "manifest" is further divided into the "mutable"and immutable" (Whorf, 1956). This is a lovely way to look at things . . . for instance, if you love me, and I love you, you will always be with me, you will not cease to be. No starting and stopping points.

J.E.B.: That is actually what our heritage is about, right? We are everything our ancestors have ever been—they are here with us. Changes there may be over time, but there is no stopping point.

C.E.M.: They say that many native American and African cultures do not show an explicit idea of duration in their languages. But language does not always reflect thought. There is more to thought and emotion than that expressed in verbal language. I think this is really important for us to keep in mind.

K.E.Y.: I remember a beautiful poem from a book on the Taos Pueblo (Wood, 1974):

> We are not important.
> Our lives are simply threads
> Pulling along the lasting thoughts
> Which travel through time that way. (p. 45)

B.H.L.: That reminds me of a story for children—*Annie and the Old One,* a very touching story (Miles, 1971) of a young girl and her grandmother whose time has come.

G.M.H.: Right. I wonder whether those people do not actually have a far more profound sense of duration than ours. It's a difficult one for us to grasp and for our language to handle, but it is there.

L.L.D.: We don't know for sure, because we don't know! We can't interpret what they are experiencing, because only they can translate parts of that experience. We can only put our own interpretations on it, and here we are limited by our conceptual system.

J.E.B.: The castle we have built protects our kingdom, but it also isolates us from the rest.

G.M.H.: That's an interesting way to put it! Probably more apt than even you yourself thought, because we tend to visualize time in space terms.

D.H.B.: Yes, Piaget (1971), among others, emphasized that. Children must somehow construct this notion of time on the basis of their understanding of movement through space, of motions and their speeds, you know. The concept of space is the more fundamental.

L.L.D.: In our culture we build a spatial image of the past, present, and future on a straight line and then conceptualize duration as the interval between two given points on that continuum.

O.L.D.: That interval is not well scaled, however. An equal unit is not there. This has come out very vividly in my experience with both children and adults using the "Man, A Course of Study" lifeline (Bruner, 1968). First, you ask children to list ten important events in their lives and then to place them on a lifeline. An interesting thing is that they uniformly order these events equidistantly on the line. The birth is typically away from the end of the string, and the most recent event is put right near the other end. It is as if they did not anticipate any future.

N.J.G.: Are you talking about a great range in age?

O.L.D.: I've used this with grade three through adults.

H.F.D.: And you get the same results?

O.L.D.: The same phenomenon is repeated.

S.D.C.: They don't put death on there?

O.L.D.: No, and I believe that's because they don't conceive of having to experience death themselves, or they don't anticipate that important event in their life.

H.F.D.: I am curious about this equidistance thing. The same length of string between two events is clearly an abstraction of the comparative importance of these life experiences, not an abstraction of the precise temporal interval.

M.M.M.: I just don't think we perceive . . . we don't measure anything that happens in our life with physical precision.

C.L.W.: Some seconds can seem like hours.

H.F.D.: Right, but it may also be that the linear model forces people to represent their experiences that way, even when they don't really think of them linearly. What Hall (1969, 1977) calls the "monochronic vs. polychronic" perspectives on time come in here. Even when individuals do not perceive and handle time as a segmented, i.e., sectionally marked or scheduled, ribbon extending straight from the past to the future, or as a commodity that can be saved, spent, wasted, made up, or what have you, the whole culture is rigidly monochronic and demands their conforming to this way of life. Polychronic cultures of, say, Southern Europe, Latin America, or the Middle East do not compartmentalize time and space as we do—many things take place simultaneously, not one thing at a time, and people are much more closely involved with each other.

S.D.C.: We can only represent as well as our representational facilities let us, is that a part of the story? That may also apply to children's drawings. Their perceptions may not necessarily change as they grow older, but the expressions of these perceptions may change because of the increased or different representational capabilities.

D.H.B.: Suppose you could give them something else, something other than a string, to represent life? What could we use?

N.J.G.: I suggest that a spiral would be usable or a circular kind of thing. We seldom try these out.

C.E.M.: Even with a string, you don't have to hold it straight and taut. It can be a curve of one sort or another.

H.F.D.: The result we observe may be a function of the instructions we give or of our interpretation. Are we really seeing what we are asking for?

O.L.D.: I don't know. These are good questions for exploration. Let's take another example though. When children are given a series of dates to order on a time line, they will most likely arrange them equidistantly on it. There may be vast differences in between these dates, e.g., 1713, 1795, 1846, and so on, but they will be distributed evenly.

J.E.B.: That's right. Even when you draw the time line on the blackboard with these dates in the right place, they will "reproduce" it in their own book with the dates evenly spaced.

H.F.D.: What is known about children's behavior regarding number lines where the numbers are not equidistant? Would they be inclined to sense that property, that mathematical property?

O.L.D.: If it's labeled mathematics, they might. If it's labeled "My life," "My father," or something like that, I don't think they would. Well, I honestly don't know. That's another good question.

H.F.D.: A lot of that is learned, I think. For example, when we represent scores in percentiles, we tend to make the intervals equally distant in our thoughts. Actually in terms of the original scores, the intervals are not of the same distance. We equalize, and we learn that.

G.M.H.: Letters in the alphabet are equally spaced. Chairs and seats in an auditorium are equally spaced. Children may be learning this underlying theme only too well.

L.M.B.: I wonder what the Hopi would do with the string, the lifeline?

O.L.D.: I don't have the slightest idea, but that's a fascinating question.

H.F.D.: We have cultures, or at least we did have, where time was, say, when the flood came. Time was when the crucifixion occurred and so on. That time didn't exist in the units of astronomical time.

N.J.G.: That's importance, again. The individual markers are important, the physical distance or interval is not.

L.M.B.: You know, that sort of difference between psychological and physical interpretations of time is not necessarily cross-cultural in nature. It can be seen among different generations within our own culture. For instance, a recent study of the ways children strike out on their own (leaving the family of orientation, taking up an occupation, getting married, or establishing a family of procreation) pointed out that these transitions to adult roles today follow a more institutionalized, and hence ordered, sequence more rigidly and uniformly than in the nineteenth century. As a result, the voluntary elements in the experience are fewer, and the whole thing is accomplished over a shorter period of time in a young person's life. "'Timely' action to nineteenth-century families consisted of helpful response in times of trouble; in the twentieth century, timeliness connotes adherence to a schedule" (Modell, Furstenberg, and Hershberg, 1976, p. 30).

D.H.B.: I wonder if a pie would work better for slices of time.

B.H.L.: Last year I asked an elementary class to show, on a pie graph, how they spend their time during the day. Very few children didn't try to divide the pie up equally, even though the distribution was something like 20 percent for playing, 6 percent for sleeping, then school, and whatever. It was still pretty evenly divided up, even though they were putting a different amount of time in each activity. I even showed them a similar pie graph, proportionately divided, and discussed it with them. But when they divide up their own, they'll do it equally.

N.J.G.: I guess it's the matter of functions, activities, or events. In the kindergarten, for instance, children's days are structured into the "serious time," "sharing time," "play time," "work time," "rest time," "clean-up time," and whatnot. It does not matter specifically when these begin or how long they last. Every event carries the same valence for children.

S.D.C.: Even though children further differentiate among those "time" units in terms of their favorites, the play time or the time just before dinner is the best time of the day, or something like that. It's not the physical attributes that count, but children's feelings about things.

L.L.D.: Salient events, people, places, as markers.

M.M.M.: A sort of related observation here. I have been studying the history of the Kiowa nation a little and found it interesting to note that what we may consider to be major events, e.g., when they were defeated by the U. S. Army, were not what they considered major events. They considered what everyone in the tribe is most likely to know as an important event to mark the month, for instance, a horse was stolen. Months were in terms of units, or moons, and these moon cycles were recorded around stories of their major events. Things that we consider the most important aspects of their history were not so to them at all.

G.M.H.: That's interesting. As *they* see it, right?

M.M.M.: As *they* see it.

TO ROAM THE EARTH

J.E.B.: What we have been talking about applies equally well to space, doesn't it?

O.L.D.: Right. The concept of space itself has changed drastically in our own culture within the past 250 years. I think that the invention of a device called the sextant in 1732 started this transformation to the so-called "scientific" representation of space in our modern maps. These may be scientific, but that's not the way most children and adults perceive their life-space.

H.D.D.: Very true. Children do not understand their neighborhood in terms of an aerial photograph taken from a space satellite. Their views are on the earth's surface, looking around themselves, looking out. Again, places and people of salience. We go from one landmark to the next; these are significant, but the paths between them are not that important.

O.L.D.: Geographers call those landmarks "nodes," I think. Nodes in a network.

C.L.W.: One of the things we typically do in the first or second grade is to ask children to map their neighborhoods. That may very well be one of the most difficult tasks there is, not because children at that age are incapable of forming coherent mental maps, but because most boys and girls nowadays don't know who lives on the other side of the street—not only across the street, but behind their house and all over. It's exasperating, particularly in modern apartment living.

B.H.L.: That's right. Their neighborhood is not only fractionated, but also vertical. We don't have a conventional way to describe that nonhorizontal neighborhood.

O.L.D.: There is also the matter of exploration. Geographers use the word "range" to describe this. What is the distance that one is able to go away from the home base? How far do today's children go in that kind of neighborhood?

G.M.H.: Not much, unless they live in a very secure suburban or rural setting.

M.M.M.: From a curriculum standpoint, and in recognition of the realities of today, how do we give kids the chance to explore neighborhoods legitimately? How do we provide the kind of hands-on or direct experience with the next block and still the next one? Or up and down?

S.D.C.: That's a tough challenge.

L.L.D.: Don't you think though, that the neighborhood in the minds of us educators is not the same as that in the minds of children? Because of social shifts and all that, their life-space is quite extended in many ways, but not necessarily in the familiar, close-in sense. They may not know people right around them, but the people, places, and events of significance to them are far-flung beyond the geographically-bound neighborhoods of ours. We may have to change our own ideas here.

B.H.L.: You are making an interesting point. We seldom deal with the geography of the grocery store or church or swimming pool or what have you—the patterns of children's purposeful interaction with people of significance at definite sites.

M.M.M.: It is still a neighborhood, but what composes the neighborhood may be quite different. Even the fact of high density (but hopefully not crowding) would give this new neighborhood a different character.

C.E.M.: That distinction between high density and crowding is an important one, not only in the neighborhood but also in the classroom. For example, when I started teaching, I taught a class of about 50 fourth graders in a small room in a large Midwestern metropolis. There were certainly times when we felt crowded, yet other times we did not feel crowded. It largely depended upon what we were doing.

H.F.D.: The relative character of space, so to speak? Objectively in terms of activities taking place in that space, and subjectively in terms of perceptions about space.

H.D.D.: I believe it is important for us to think not only how we get more space, but also about how we utilize that space. In other words, how to use space in ways that free children rather than in ways that limit them. In many classrooms, children nowadays have a lot of space. Six feet this way, and six feet that way, you know. What often happens, though, is that they are isolated by that space, kind of imprisoned by it, if you know what I mean.

G.M.H.: Right! Some of the most crowded rooms I have ever seen were good places for kids to be, while some of the rooms with the least visible crowding had, in fact, the largest amount of invisible, hidden sort of control.

H.D.D.: It's more the human factor that's there, and how things are managed for the people who are there.

D.H.B.: Not only *for* the people, but also *by* the people. For instance, children do adjust their interpersonal positions and actions to accommodate a higher density.

J.E.B.: Also, when we talk about space, we typically refer only to the floor space, forgetting the vertical dimension, what goes up from the floor, what comes down from the ceiling. Then there are hallways and outdoors—all that kind of space, seldom used, or planfully used.

H.D.D.: I think a whale of a lot of space in classrooms is wasted because of too much furniture, particularly individual desks. Yet, if you look at it from the other side, that may be the only thing in school that a child has as his or her own. So, we have conflicting demands on space.

B.H.L.: That's important. Children must have some kind of personal area where they could get away from others. Then, of course, there are times when they have to be with other people, even in direct physical contact.

S.D.C.: The feeling of security or of "This is mine." A reference point. An anchor.

M.M.M.: I don't know whether children would need "my own space" so much, if all the rest of it didn't belong to the teacher or other authority. They may have to have something that's their own, because there isn't anything else in school over which they have any real control. For most young children, the same function can be served by, say, just a little basket bearing their name, or something.

C.L.W.: I think the key phrase is, "there isn't anything else in school over which they have any real say." The real issue is that of control over one's own fate, be it in space terms or time terms. Children honestly don't have much control over their life, especially in school.

B.H.L.: You are so right. This year I have been working extra hard and having my sixth graders work extra hard, and classroom life became tedious and discouraging. Attendance was down, partially due to colds and flu, but I also felt that it was due to the lack of joy in our days. So I eased up and decided to let the children just "be" more, not necessarily "do" more. We now have four periods of time during the day when it is really their show—the "talking time," noon "game period," "uninterrupted sustained silent reading period (USSR)," and a "personal project time." The last one is at the end of the day, and almost anything goes on with only one condition: it really matters personally to the child, and the child puts forth the effort and concentration on his or her "thing"—sketches on the theme, cartoon collections, models, journals and the like. The difference has been amazing! Perfect attendance, with some children coming to school who should really have stayed in bed. A better tone to the day, for me and for them. Oh, yes, I have also set aside the last part of the day on Fridays for the class to use as they wish . . . within reason. Things are much better.

N.J.G.: Fascinating! What are they going to do this coming Friday?

B.H.L.: Learn how to do Cossack dancing! That's their idea and a take-off from social studies.

M.M.M.: How are you going to manage that?

B.H.L.: I have been able to ask a nearby college to send someone to show us. Thank goodness! I would have never thought of Russian dancing for that period!

C.E.M.: That's very interesting. I just want to say that that same feeling of self-determination, or my "own thing" feeling, may be found in children's dreams. Certainly not physical, but these can also give them their own space in the mental sense. Most teachers actively discourage children from creating that space. "Daydreams" and "fantasies" are dirty words!

M.M.M.: Yes, even "meditation." Actually such self-reflection is very necessary and constructive in the classroom.

G.M.H.: When a child is looking out the window, the teacher typically gets concerned because the child is not attending. In fact, the child may be attending productively to his or her individual quest. Not in the group sense, to be sure, but the child's own world is not to be denied, at least at that moment.

C.L.W.: Often, if you ask them what they're thinking about, it turns out to be better than what's going on in the group!

M.M.M.: A part of this is one's ability to be alone, to be with oneself. That goes against the cultural grain, it seems. Like a snail pulling itself inside a shell. You become involved in yourself in this sense, and you build your own space. It doesn't really matter what the physical space is like.

N.J.G.: It's also your own time in that, very sense.

M.M.M.: That's right.

L.L.D.: Isn't that withdrawal though? A regressive action?

M.M.M.: Yes, it is withdrawal, but I am not arguing for withdrawal in total. Children, and all of us, have to have time to withdraw. I, for one, resent it very much if I am forced in a whole group of people to be always concerned about what everybody else is concerned about, actively doing and thinking what everybody else is thinking and doing. So, for self-preservation, I'll take myself off. We need that time, we need that withdrawal.

D.H.B.: Even in the case of those children who have been defined as emotionally disturbed, this may indeed be the healthiest adjustment they could make at that particular time, given their life's circumstances. Moustakas (1959) was making the same point—for a long time, he felt as though withdrawal was a maladaptive response but, for many children, at their particular time, that was what they needed to do.

L.M.B.: This also ties in with the whole experience of creation and creativity. Remember the concept of "regression in the service of the ego" (Kris, 1952)? It is a very healthy sort of regression that is prerequisite of any creative endeavors.

S.D.C.: I am reminded of an Oriental proverb here. To catch a paper dragon, one should not grasp very actively for it. That will make it move farther away from you. Be still, and let it come to you, or something like that. We must be receptive.

N.J.G.: After saying all that about one's mental space, there still seems a basic need for a territory of your own, no matter how small or big. That spatial envelope, that protective bubble.

J.E.B.: There is that kind of thing on the playground, you know. This is the third-grade part, and that is the sixth-grade boys' place for baseball and nobody else's.

N.J.G.: You earlier mentioned hallways as typically left unused, but there are corners that belong to certain groups. At least in high school, each gang's territory is staked out, a section of hallway right next to certain lockers, for instance. There are definite territorial boundaries.

C.L.W.: Some bathrooms too.

J.E.B.: And entrances to the school.

G.M.H.: Have there been studies on all that?

H.F.D.: No, I don't think so, particularly in relation to implications for education as such, and to action suggestions for teachers. There are some references of interest though (Barker and Gump, 1964; Jacobs, 1961; Richardson, 1967; White, 1953).

THE HUMAN CONTACT

H.D.D.: I am very sure that systematic studies will uphold the value of those spaces and things kids can crawl into, climb onto, hang from, sit upon or what have you.

S.D.C.: That's a part of the need for exploration, which has to be in a delicate balance with the need for attachment to encourage the development of competence in a child.

C.L.W.: To explore and appreciate space in relation to one's self, right? There are some good classroom exercises for that purpose (Castillo, 1974; Way, 1967).

K.E.Y.: To create, explore, appreciate, and recreate, I guess. Physically and mentally.

C.E.M.: That goes along with the idea of letting children have more responsibility for their lives. We teachers tend to make ourselves responsible for kids and all of their time. Back to Sweden for an example. When attending ninth grade there, my son was responsible for certain portions of his school day. He controlled these and learned how to manage the time.

H.F.D.: How was it different, specifically, from our situation?

C.E.M.: Well, he could come and go from the school, more or less as he pleased. There were some things established—students were told what activities were going on at certain times. In the beginning of his program, he told them what he was interested in, and they suggested to him, "Alright, that's fine, but maybe you would be interested in these, too." It was a discussion, a give-and-take planning, and he felt he was coming up with the answer instead of their directing him all the way. He was very active in these planned things. They let him have some free choices and otherwise free movement.

L.L.D.: Free movement?

C.E.M.: Exactly. He didn't have to have a pass to go to the hall for an interval or to go to the lavatory. They trusted him as an individual, and they obviously start this at a very early age there.

B.H.L.: Come to think of it, it is rather strange that with young children here we permit them to have a lot more movement than older children. Actually, as you grow older, you should be better able to deal with space, your own as well as others', if you're learning space. Yet our schools seem to go the opposite way. Then when they get to college, all of a sudden they are let go.

S.D.C.: On the assumption that they can handle space and time. How to arrange one's life, literally. Setting up schedules, keeping appointments, maintaining a place for living and working, getting a career bearing, pacing one's activities, and much more.

K.E.Y.: How they manage all that has not been closely examined. Just a bit of information on what seems to happen in residence halls (Chickering, 1974) or library (Sommer, 1969), but not yet terribly practical in nature.

G.M.H.: You know, having a large school with plenty of room doesn't do you a lot of good if you're not allowed out of your cage.

J.E.B.: "Cage" is an interesting expression to use there and, unfortunately, appropriate in many instances.

H.D.D.: We have to open that cage, and that applies to the whole school, not only to each classroom.

L.M.B.: Also, children ought to be having many more adults available to them throughout the day, not just teachers.

B.H.L.: Right, we need more people, all sorts of people, in the lives of children. It's teacher some of the time, and other people some of the time. The school's got to be not just in this building, restricted in space, but all over the place, all across the community.

L.M.B.: Lots of older folks, for instance. Many with broad visions and fine skills to share. Children's experiences need to include close interactions with people of many different ages. That adds to intergenerational understanding and to the development of the sense of interdependence.

C.E.M.: For instance, they have been actually setting up, in

Sweden, housing developments that include both day care centers and apartments for the aged. Parks are so structured that the young and the old can interact with each other for the amount of time either can stand.

J.E.B.: Many teachers here have also been trying to bring older people into the classroom to be with children or to show them how certain things are done. The results can be very good for both, but the system must change its time-and-space framework to maximize the benefits.

D.H.B.: What do you mean?

J.E.B.: For example, saying that the elderly can't go to day care centers because, when they come, they can stay for only so long within their tolerance. That means so much moving here, there, and back, and the current institutional framework cannot accommodate that. The aged have to fit the frame, or they go, they stay out.

C.L.W.: The form must be maintained—forget about the function. That's all too familiar.

L.M.B.: Understanding different styles of life and working out a mutually functional schedule are often impossible under such circumstances. So people stand isolated, feeling unneeded and worthless.

B.H.L.: Everyone feeling lonely and miserable, confined within one's own fears and uncertainties. That's sad.

O.L.D.: I have a married son who is a teacher now. One of his most powerful early experiences was when, at about age ten, he went with a Cub Scout pack to a retirement home. He can still visualize that place, not a dirty, smelly kind of thing, but *lonely!* He even today says, "Dad, nobody, but nobody goes to see these people!"

G.M.H.: Sympathy but also fear. I can remember as a Girl Scout going and singing in old people's homes and feeling very fearful. "Oh, no, I never want to be like this!" I was so sad about it and felt very uncomfortable around these folks.

M.M.M.: But if well handled, that sort of awareness may be very constructive. Through their vulnerability, the elderly show us that we are vulnerable. They are us!

K.E.Y.: Adults taking time to talk with children about those feelings of sadness or fear or what have you would be very helpful.

D.H.B.: Or just closely listening to them when they are ready to speak. That, as we know, can be most any time, often totally unexpected and mixed in with other things of seeming irrelevance. That sort of listening may be a rare gift, but every teacher should at least try to cultivate whatever little he or she has been given.

H.F.D.: That interaction would be critical, I believe. Without that, we will exist only in our own lives without much appreciation of human continuity and commonality.

G.M.H.: Both within and across generations, right? If there were no past, there would be no history and perhaps no future. We run the risk of being confined merely to the isolated slice of the present.

M.M.M.: Without good hindsight and insight, we won't have any foresight, right?

L.L.D.: And we find people at the two ends of the continuum "useless," both the very young and the very old.

C.L.W.: You can add to the list adolescents. They are "useless" in the production sense.

L.M.B.: Also the group between young adulthood and retirement, say, ages between 25 and 65. They may be "productive," but no one's paying much attention to them in a human sense. How they grow and struggle, you know.

H.D.D.: That's just about everybody then, isn't it? Who's left?

H.F.D.: That's precisely the point. Everyone would be isolated and forgotten, unless we become aware that we are one. The bell tolls for all.

N.J.G.: You know, if we figure out what needs to be done and ask who can do which aspects of these tasks well, we will stand a better chance of getting everyone involved. Working together, and through that coming to know each other. Instead of categorizing people by age, labeling them, and then excluding them from the scene.

B.H.L.: That also applies to the interaction among children of different ages. Even though some efforts have been made in recent years (Allen, 1976; Gartner, Kohler, and Riessman, 1971), our age-graded schooling does not encourage young ones and older students working and playing together.

H.D.D.: Right, some contrast with, say, the Russian system (Bronfenbrenner, 1970) or Summerhill (Neill, 1960).

B.H.L.: We are not saying that we ought to pull clear out of the situation as a teacher and say, "O.K., you decide," or "What would you like?," are we?

L.L.D.: No, of course not. We have to be there to monitor the whole process of decision-making, action, and follow-through. We must be asking questions like, "Would that be satisfactory in terms of these other things?" "Have you thought of those matters?" "What about these people?" or "Would there be some other ways we might do this rather than the first idea that came up?"

S.D.C.: Right. There is an important difference between the teacher being involved in the decision-making as a contributing member of the group and the teacher throwing up her hands, saying, "Oh, that's for you. Anything you decide is O.K. by me."

B.H.L.: Children need a teacher who acts as a responsible adult, not as an overgrown kid. The teacher is an example, for better or for worse, of the adult community.

D.H.B.: A teacher's responsibility is to be authentic, not to be nobody and nothing.

G.M.H.: That's a shared responsibility, shared among all of us, across time and space.

K.E.Y.: Well put. You know, I come back to this thought time and again. When we discuss children, we cannot help discussing ourselves. We end up finding us examining ourselves. In a sense, children are the medium through which we study ourselves, a mirror in which we see ourselves. Hopefully, readers of this book will join us in taking another look and facing that mutual responsibility seriously.

L.M.B.: Right. We have been discussing lots of things in this retreat. We don't have answers, but we are asking questions. We are searching, and that process of search is the one we wish to share with our friends and colleagues.

K.E.Y.: Let's close the meeting on that note.

In life, what is important is often intangible. The obvious, formal curriculum of school may therefore have little to do with the subtle yet powerful teaching of cultural fundamentals through the total experience of schooling. This chapter, prepared by a teacher educator, examines the how of this hidden curriculum as it relates to time and space.

Rituals of the Hidden Curriculum

NATHALIE J. GEHRKE

Teachers have probably always realized that though they taught a planned curriculum to their students, they were also influencing the lives of those students by the way they taught them, that is, by the hidden curriculum. Routines of the classroom, often established to facilitate orderly administration of daily activities, form a major unit of this hidden curriculum. Through daily routines students become habituated to the desired activities and to methods of utilizing time and space. Lining up for entrance and exit from the classroom, recitation and drill, and seating assignments have taken on a ritualized character in many classrooms.

Now, the difference between routine and ritual is that ritual is symbolic of the participants' belief in a power beyond human experience. For children this belief is quite simplistic; ritual behavior demonstrates acceptance of a superhuman or supraindividual power. Taking part in classroom ritual helps students gain a sense of enduringness and power, much as Erikson (1963) suggests they achieve through play. I remember a particular procedure from my own elementary school days that may help illustrate what I mean by a classroom ritual. Early each morning the teacher would pass gravely up and down the rows examining our hands and handkerchiefs. No guilt was greater than that we felt when charged with dirty hands or "hankylessness." We were very cocky and self-assured when we could display relatively clean hands—first palms down, then palms up—on top of a neatly folded (never to be used) handkerchief. We were thoroughly convinced that cleanliness (or at least its appearance) was next to godliness.

The stability and feeling of competence experienced when one has performed a ritual well are compelling incentives for further performance. At the same time, strong moral sanctions are imposed on those who perform poorly or not at all. In other words, it becomes "sinful" not to comply with the rituals; a sense not only of power, but of "rightness" prevails when one has.

Gluckman (1962), an anthropologist, has said that, "Rituals of all kinds are associated with efforts to ensure success and avoid disaster" (p. 31), and this is certainly no less true of the rituals of the classroom than those of any other human groups. To avoid the imagined or real disaster of anarchy, classroom groups ritualize their activities with varying degrees of formality. At their least formal, classroom rituals include special etiquette, observance of social distance, and avoidance of specified subjects of conversation. For example, one never addresses the teacher by *first* name or inquires about age. One rarely discusses the teacher's home life. The most formal, and more easily recognized, are the ceremonialized observances of the opening and closing of the school day, special holidays, and patriotic expressions.

Formal and informal rituals are subtly and openly taught from the time the child enters a nursery or preschool. Expectations of performance are increased as the students pass from grade to grade, but actual focus on the rituals may decrease. It is not unusual, for instance, for a first grade teacher to view the first weeks of class primarily as a time to get pupils used to the routines with little or no emphasis on subject matter and skills. Adams and Biddle (1970) reported that first grade teachers spent more time talking about organizational topics than any other teachers. Upper elementary teachers would be appalled, however, if that were *all* they had done by the end of the same period. They expect their students to be ready "to get down to work," to know the general rituals, and to require instruction only in the idiosyncratic demands of their new teacher ("In my class you will write your name on the upper half of the right side of the back of your papers. Fold the paper in half lengthwise and place it on my desk here, and only here, at the beginning of the period!").

Many of the rituals of the classroom group do not even rise to the awareness of the group members. The rules of etiquette and procedure may be so basic to the classroom environment that they are, as Hall (1959) has explained, brought to awareness only when broken. Seldom are students told that they may not intrude on the teacher's space by rifling through the files or casually draping themselves over the desk or in the chair of the teacher. But if the crime is committed, an immediate reprimand may be received, or the offender may perceive, at the very least, a cooling of regard or increased suspicion about motives or movements.

While not all teachers would be offended by behavior of the above sort, the environment of the classroom tends to influence many teachers to behave this way. Gump (1964) described a number of studies that seem to indicate that the nature of the behavior setting may coerce teacher behavior patterns as much as teacher personality variables. Following their video tape studies of the realities of teaching, Adams and Biddle (1970) also concluded that the environment coerced teacher behavior, forcing it toward a benevolent authoritarian formality. The sense of duty and commitment expressed by teachers in regard to classroom routines indicates that they also think of them as sacred rituals of enduringness and efficacy. Transgressing peer teachers and students are described not just as "poor," but often as "bad."

The character of the rituals of the classroom group, knowingly or unknowingly established by the teacher and students, is greatly dependent on the use of time and space. It is not only important that a specific action be taken, but also that it be carried out at a prescribed time, in a prescribed place. To return to the paper example mentioned earlier, it was not only how the paper looked that was important (name on back) but that it be delivered to its proper space at the appropriate time (on the desk, at the beginning of the period).

The time and space aspects of ritual behavior are as important as are the actions performed. Children's faux pas in public, which embarrass their parents and produce peals of adult laughter, are often errors in time or place rather than totally unacceptable actions. The child who talks out loud in a church service or waves and helloes a parent in the audience from the front row of the children's chorus is not engaging in unacceptable behavior as such, but has failed to acknowledge the restrictions of time and space—not here! and not now!

Unless all members of a group observe the required time and space appropriateness in rituals, the group may become hopelessly mired in the most trivial of activities. A beginning teacher was observed whose well planned lesson was completely subverted when students began trotting to the teacher's desk to hand in their homework at carefully irregular intervals while the teacher attempted to lead a discussion.

Though we in the Western world have come to be extremely suspicious of ritualization and have abandoned many of the formal rituals of religious and secular life, they are still important factors among groups of people who must live and work together in very close quarters. The group members may be quite unaware of just how much the ritualized practices affect their day-to-day life, functioning not just to reduce hostile in-fighting and maintain an uneasy truce among group members, but actually to promote harmony and further the group's causes. Anthropologists have categorized tribal rituals according to three primary functions benefiting the group:

1. Building respect—ritualized observances of status relations between persons and social categories.
2. Smoothing social relations—ritualized observance of common interests of a social aggregate.
3. Avoiding confusion and anxiety during crises—ritualized observance in change of activities and roles.

These three categories can serve to organize a closer look at the rituals of the hidden curriculum.

STATUS RITUALS IN THE CLASSROOM

In the typical classroom "tribe" there are two major status positions: teacher and student. In addition to these, some classroom groups may include teacher aides, student teachers, and parent volunteers. These last three positions are similar to the teacher status, so for practical purposes, they are classified with teacher here. Students may also be subcategorized as good (top, or gifted) or poor (bad, slow, or unmotivated). They may be leaders or followers, trusted or untrusted. These categorizing labels give them slightly different status in some classes, but in many of the class rituals such characteristics will matter little, for the status rituals are focused primarily on building respect for the leader. To this end the teacher establishes, or is given, certain treatment by the students. One may quickly notice, for example, that while teachers are nearly always addressed formally, students are addressed with their familiar names. Beyond this matter of address are the less obvious, though highly important, matters of time and space etiquette, here discussed in terms of movement, territoriality, and time control.

Free Movement and Territory Claims

Teachers may enter the classroom space and move about it completely at will. No corner of the room is off limits to the teacher, often including the desks, trays, or cubby holes of the students. Students, on the other hand, are frequently restricted. They must not move freely, but are allowed by the teacher to move to certain areas only at times designated. To be out of one's assigned space without permission is forbidden with grave consequences for offenders. Children quickly learn to ritualize being in one's seat and can be depended upon to tattle and make judgments on others on the basis of who gets into or out of, or stays put in, seats.

It is highly unlikely that the student will enter certain territory that is tacitly acknowledged as the leader-teacher's domain, that is, the front of the room. Adams and Biddle (1970) reported:

> It seems as if the teacher has her territories too. . . . In fact during the course of our study, the teacher's sanctum—the front of the room—was invaded by active classroom members very rarely. In one

of the 32 lessons, pupil emitters were at the front of the room for 17 minutes, in three of the lessons, they were there for less than five minutes. In the other 27 classrooms the teacher maintained his or her territory inviolate. (p. 65)

The marking off of teacher territory serves to invest whomever occupies that territory with the authority of the leader status. If a student attempts to lead the student group in a teacher sanctioned activity, the person is very likely to enter the leader space at the front of the room to do so. It is probable that peers will be more willing to allow the individual to carry out the role if he or she initiates the leadership attempt from the front. Likewise, student teachers and visitors are more apt to receive the respect due the leader if they occupy the reserved territory, at least as they begin to replace the teacher. In addition, if a person aspiring to leadership moves about the room aggressively and freely, as students are not allowed to do, it is probable that that person will be deferentially treated. However, if an aspiring student leader is not respected by the others, the attempt to use the leader territory will be considered a joke or a "pain." Simply occupying the space is not sufficient. It is instead a reinforcement, an affirmation of the leader's right to lead.[1]

Not only is the person occupying the leader territory given the respect due the prime leader, but the objects that occupy the front also gain symbolic power value (Sommer, 1967). To occupy the teacher's desk, stand at the podium, or use the high stool found in some classrooms gives one power. The same objects placed outside the leader territory might still be invested with symbolic value, but less than when found at the front and center.

Teacher as Timekeeper

Control of time is also used as a symbol in the rituals for building respect for leadership. The person who determines when certain activities will begin and end is a respected individual because of that power. Success or failure on some projects, e.g., achievement tests, may well be determined by whether the timekeeper "gives" enough time for completion. That the teacher-leader has the right to

---

[1]It is interesting to speculate on where students, engaged in nonteacher sanctioned leadership attempts, place themselves in the classroom. Are rebellions literally fomented in the back row?

give or limit one's time allotment is basic. Some classes are more relaxed about this, but it is always acknowledged that any relaxation is at the discretion of the teacher.

The right to punish tardiness and reward promptness lies with the teacher. Also the power to reward students by allowing them to leave early or arrive late is given to the teacher. While the teacher controls the times of coming and going of students, no one within the group can complain too loudly if the teacher is late to class, holds the class longer than the bell, or spends time on unrelated activities, e.g., chatting in the hall with another teacher.

The leadership of the teacher in enforcing arrival and departure rules is generally supported by several key students who goad others to conform. These lieutenants are quickly enlisted at the beginning of the year by experienced teachers to assist in various ritualized aspects of the day. Even the inexperienced teacher may find these "natural" leaders coming to the rescue in support of attempts to regularize behaviors. In her "Advice to a New Teacher," one "old pro" offered this:

> If class is noisy, stop teaching. Don't teach an unsettled class. Make a point of not resuming your teaching until you have every child's attention. You will find the children who are cooperative will force the uncooperative children to fall into line.
>
> Tell children what time they are expected to arrive at school. I always insist that my children be in line at 9:45 and 12:45. This is before the bell rings. If you insist on these times, you'll find most of them will arrive on time. Again, other members of the class will discipline them. (Ilnitski, 1974, p. 127)

Whatever methods these cooperative students use to force the others "to fall in line," they are supported in their efforts by the approval of the teacher. Presumably their methods are relatively benign.

Testing the Leadership

The rituals regarding movement, territoriality, and time keeping are all rituals theoretically controlled by the teacher for the purpose of building respect for the teacher. It is assumed that if the leader is respected for the power to control the time, space, and behaviors of the student-followers, reasonable social order will prevail and "disaster will be avoided."

There is, however, at least one ritual that students rather than the teachers control. I call it the "testing the teacher" ritual. Teachers themselves are aware of this trial by transgression of space-time expectations (the "not here-not nowness" of the teacher's rules). Some of the oft repeated teaching maxims revolve around preparedness for the teacher test, e.g., "Don't smile until Christmas," "Start out tough, you can always soften later," and "Come down hard on the first kid who gets out of line." All these sage bits of advice are aimed, it seems, toward control of behaviors outside the prescribed time-space use regulations established or desired by the teacher to ensure the smooth operation of the class.

From my limited observations and experience, it appears that such teacher tests are not apt to be organized rebellions (these come later), but rather are individual infractions of the rules by an increasingly large proportion of the students. For example, during the first few days of class only a few avowed rebels may be tardy. If they go unchecked, more students join them in being tardy, then more and more. Finally even the "lieutenants" will be aware that no punishment results from late arrival. The teacher has been tested and flunked the leadership exam.

The testing occurs in other ways too, e.g., talking out of turn, sharpening a pencil, visiting during discussion or lecture, falling asleep, using furniture in unconventional manners, or wearing a hat. Notice that most of these misdemeanors are like the faux pas of small children, not inherently unacceptable behavior, just inappropriate for the time and place. Students usually try all of these with the expectation that they may be punished. If they are, or if it is otherwise made clear that such behaviors are unacceptable, the teacher can be said to have passed the leadership torture test. The students will continue to test the teacher in all areas until the limits are known and, in fact, will probably continue little pop quizzes throughout the year. But generally, most teachers feel if they make it through the first series of tests, they are pretty well established. Unfortunately, they also would probably agree that if they fail in any way during the initial test series, the whole year tends to be a loss. You are pegged as a pushover and feel helpless to control your destiny. This is most horrifying to first-year teachers, who have vivid nightmares of just such an occurence.

Even if the teacher is finally able to build sufficient respect for the leader-teacher role and obtains relative conformity in student behavior, conflicts between group members are bound to arise. They often occur because of the limited space and time of the classroom.

RITUALS FOR SOOTHING CONFLICTS

For an extended period of time, usually a nine-month block, members of a class are in extremely close contact with perhaps 30 to 35 others. In this case, "close contact" is not simply a figure of speech, but an accurate description of the scene. Most classrooms are crowded. Jackson (1968) remarked on the fact that few, if any, other situations in life require so many people to remain so close for such long sessions and that such crowding cannot but affect the learning and the quality of life in that place. Lehmann (1960), writing on the environment of the classroom, complained about the lack of research on the effects this crowding may have on the learning of children. Even in the most ideal of classrooms, children are frequently elbow to elbow in work areas with no opportunity to withdraw to an office or lounge for privacy. Study carrels and quiet corners are arranged by some thoughtful teachers for their students, but private territory in a crowded space is most unlikely.

It seems worth noting that schools provide private or semi-private places for students' material possessions, yet none for the students themselves. Though they are a retreat of sorts, even the restrooms lack privacy. In some schools any doors originally installed in the restrooms have been removed to prevent sneak smoking. Unfortunately, the effect is to reduce private space and time.

The crowded condition of even the most ideal classroom almost demands that much of the group activity be routinized for orderly accomplishment of the prescribed tasks. Then the routines become ritualized and imbued with a certain sacred air to further reduce transgressions, hostility, and confusion in the crowd. Rituals in the common interest occur in the open-space classroom as well as in the self-contained classroom. Without an untransgressable pattern for organizing daily activity, confusion and bunching, lost time, and bickering are expected to occur.

Whose Turn Is It?

Some rituals of the common interest are readily observable, as are the roles of time and space in them. Look, for instance, at the ritual of taking turns. Taking turns requires that each person uses the objects or space for a limited time, then relinquishes the activity, objects, or space to another, after which the person waits a pre-scribed time or sequence before having another turn. There is prob-ably no procedure in the classroom that is more heavily sanctioned or more strongly inculcated than this principle of taking turns. It is one that is taught first by the family, then constantly reinforced in everything from restroom use to playground games, and even to college advising.

In both open-space and self-contained classrooms students must take turns using equipment, using passes, sharpening pencils, going to the library, and talking to the teacher. It matters little that one person may need more utilization time in a particular area, or that one may need to use an object or space several times at unevenly spaced intervals. The rules must stand in the common interest of the group. Some may suffer a bit, but it is assumed that the majority will be served.

Perhaps no other breach of etiquette is likely to provoke anger more quickly in the classroom group than someone not taking turns, either by not relinquishing the space and objects when the time is up or by sneaking in extra turns out of sequence. This unfairness is likely to be tattled to the teacher (the turn enforcer) who must remind, reprimand, or punish according to the degree of seriousness of the transgression. One who won't take turns is morally corrupt! The strong moral overtones to space and time turn-taking are car-ried throughout life by most of us. Who has not bristled at the person who cuts in line at the supermarket or bank; who has not muttered at those who refuse to alternate as two car lines merge, or at those who take longer at the drinking fountain than everyone else.

Of course this turn-taking does not apply to the teacher, who may at any time interrupt the turn-taking of students to use the equip-ment, space, or time of the students "in line." It is acknowledged by the group that teacher time is more valuable and therefore shortcuts may be allowed. Teachers are privileged to go to the front of the lunch line (or have their own line), to call for the scissors when needed, not when available, or to use the restroom whenever desired. This privilege sets the teacher leader apart from the group and builds respect as well as generally serving the common interest. Since the teacher does lead the other group members in activities, it may, indeed, be important for the group that she or he be able to take shortcuts in order to keep the group as a whole from losing time. Complaints about teacher shortcuts are more apt to deal with how they are done, not on whether they may be taken. A pushy, arrogant teacher is seldom a favorite with students, or with anyone else for that matter.

The Ritual of the Raised Hand

One ritual of turn-taking, which deserves attention in its own right, is the ritual of the raised hand. Raising the hand to be called on is an institution in the classroom. It is a method for signalling the desire to control a time period to speak, to answer or ask a question, or to be given the freedom to move or change activity. It is an expected practice to lower the hand when another has been called on first, and it is considered silly, rude, or overly zealous to persist in raising one's hand after another has been designated to receive a turn. (I have observed students working individually who take a break from activity by raising their hands when they know the teacher is busy with others. As long as the arm is raised, it will appear that the student can't proceed without help and is therefore free to be disengaged. Some individuals have become extremely proficient at raising their hands for long periods of time while conversing nonchalantly with a neighbor whose hand is also raised.)

While on the surface it would appear that the raised hand ritual equalizes a student's opportunity to use air time or space, it is often not so. Equality of opportunity for the student rests with the teacher, since the teacher may or may not acknowledge the raised hand. Though most teachers attempt to be fair in this procedure and call on different students, the very environment of the classroom may coerce a certain pattern of awareness of upraised hands. Adams and Biddle (1970) found a restricted corridor of teacher-student communication in their studies of conventionally organized classrooms.

Teachers called on and received nearly all responses from students in the very front row and in a line down the middle of the room. Others outside this "T" area received few, if any, questions or solicitations of participation from the teacher. This suggests that though some equalization of attention is derived from the raised hand ritual, its function is more probably the reduction of confusion and hostile jockeying for time and position among the group members. Children may eventually learn to choose seats in the classroom space that put them in or out of the "T" corridor of attention and consequently increase or decrease their hand raising acknowledgment and participation. This space choice, far from equalizing opportunity, supports a kind of hierarchy of peers that lets each student know her or his place, even if that place means near invisibility in the group.

That each person has a place spatially and socially appears to be an important method for keeping harmony in the group (Sommer, 1969). Teachers in the early grades frequently make use of the assigned place to maintain order. A child who is in some way disrupting the class may be ordered to return to an assigned desk or a spot on the floor. This isolates the offender from the other students so that they will not be tainted or harmed. Such a punishment may be increased by making the guilty party put his or her head down, an act of contrition that, in effect, isolates the offender even further.

Promoting Efficiency and Honesty

The common interest rituals for handing in and handing back assignments, for engaging in various learning activities, e.g., recitation and drill, and for evaluation activities are all dependent to varying degrees on the structuring of time and space in relation to the activity. If handing in papers is to be nondisruptive to the group, a quick, efficient method must be found to deliver them to the teacher. Penalties are often given for failure to follow the prescribed method and though there may be grumblings about the penalties, there is seldom a revolt of any proportion. Students have learned over time that protocol is often as important as content.

Teachers have variously ritualized paper collection and distribution. Some deliver and receive material as part of the opening ritual of class. Others prefer the end of a period. Some have the papers brought to them, others collect the homework as they walk among the students or send a delegate to do so. Some teachers require that the papers be stacked a certain way from person to person and row to row so that they may be rapidly returned after reading. This is often accompanied by alphabetical seating for increased efficiency. Such near mechanical precision in ritual may also extend to the paper heading, sheet size, folding method, and staple placement.

Elementary and secondary teachers are not the only ones who may become overly zealous in demanding ritualized precision on this paper matter. In fact, the requirements seem to become even more stringent as the student advances. Witness to this are the imperatives issued to graduate students as "guidelines" for thesis or dissertation format ("I'm sorry we can't accept that even if it makes sense. If we let you do that, everyone will want an exception to the rule!").

At no time, however, are there more rigid specifications for behavior than during examinations. Failure to carry out the rituals for test-taking can provoke a severe response from the leader and group members. Testing is heavily saturated with morality. Beginning with the child's earliest testing experiences and progressing to the comprehensive examinations of graduate students, the test is the supreme proving ground for honesty, a large part of which is again a matter of appropriateness of actions in time and space.

Time limits are often strictly enforced during testing. Students are signalled when they may begin and when they must stop working. They are sometimes required to work on segments of the exam during specified blocks of time. Starting too soon or working longer than the allotted time can result in penalties as severe as automatic failure of the examination.

Space factors are also rigidly controlled. The usual seating arrangement may be altered. Sometimes, if space permits, students are required to leave empty seats between them to reduce the possibility of cheating (intruding one's eyes on another's personal space in which lies the test paper). Teachers often monitor the test by taking what Adams and Biddle (1970) refer to as "the Grand Tour," down the middle corridor and around the boundaries of the students' desks. The teacher's movements through the group space are apparently designed not only to offer help, but also to reduce the temptation any of the members may feel to help each other or to help themselves.

Some teachers seem to become more enamoured of the testing

protocol than interested in the evaluation outcome, but most testing procedures can, again, be traced to the common interest of the group. In attempts to ensure everyone a fair chance to do one's best, confusion about procedure must be minimized. The more any potentially disruptive elements are controlled through sacred routine, the greater the chance for equalized opportunity and harmony among group members.

All for One and One for All

In addition to rituals to reduce confusion in the group, there are rituals that primarily serve to unify the group and promote a sense of belonging. While elementary teachers probably employ more belonging rituals than upper-grade teachers, evidence may be seen at all levels. Birthday celebrations are among the most common sharing and unifying activities. No matter what a student's status among peers, the individual becomes special on a birthday and is fêted grandly or modestly as is the custom in that group. The celebrant may be allowed special privileges, for instance, free time, which is seldom considered a right.

The class group is often unified by preparation for special holidays and by school competitions, especially in athletics and money-making endeavors. During these events space and time of the classroom are used by the group to make a statement about its cohesion. The decoration of the classroom may be undertaken by the teacher alone, but if a group spirit is the goal, the project will probably be cooperatively carried out by all the class members. The amount of time allotted for preparation and celebration of holidays and special events and contests may be one relatively good indication of the teacher's interest in making individual students feel like contributing members of the group.

A crowd of indistinguishable souls, whether young or old, can quickly turn to a mob when there are no procedures for helping each person establish a sense of individual worth and a share in the group's welfare. Crowded schools would appear to be ripe for mob action because many are so large and the students so alienated. We should probably be surprised not that students do engage in mob behavior from time to time, but that they do so so rarely. This rarity may be due not only to use of cohesion-building rituals, but also to the use of rituals for confusion and anxiety avoidance—what I call crisis control.

RITUALS FOR CRISIS CONTROL

The close quarters and large size of the classroom group are most sorely tested during times of transition. The entrances and exits, openings and closing, and changes in activity or subject matter can be times of absolute chaos if all group members proceed in their own styles. Ritualization becomes a method for crisis control and the reduction of group member anxiety.

Rituals of transition, called *rites de passage* by anthropologists, are among the most frequently documented of group rituals. They have been observed to occur during critical changes in status, e.g., birth, puberty, marriage, death, and during critical movements, such as when the individual or group travels in and out of the tribe's domain. *Rites de passage* have been divided into three observable though sometimes overlapping parts: *separation* from the old state of things; a *marginal* period; and an *aggregation* to a new condition, all of which aim toward reduction of the harmful effects of the transition.

Rites for Coming and Going

If the rites of the classroom change are broken down using these three categories, the function of time and space in them can be discerned. Consider, for example, the period of transition from one activity to another. Whatever the students may have been doing is halted and closed (separation stage). At a signal or directive from the teacher or the bell, equipment and books are put away, the material covered is summarized, and last minute exhortations are given on homework or future work. There is then a transition or marginal period when students may mill around or return to their desks to wait quietly (or not so quietly) until directions are forthcoming about the new activity (aggregation). Once directions have been given, equipment procured, and work area placement finalized, students are ready to engage in the new activity. Some teachers are able to accomplish these transitions with a minimum of time expended, while others may wash around with their students for large blocks of time in a state of marginality. Unless students have come to think of that routine behavior as the right way to act, individual styles will prevail, and the time for concentration on the planned curriculum may be shortened.

Of course the process of entering or leaving the classroom itself is a rite of passage. In elementary schools in many areas there is a signal for closure of activity and subsequent scurrying and putting away, a period of lining up for exit led by line leaders, and a filing out and dispersion period as the teacher reviews the procession. Looking once again at the advice of the "old pro" for confirmation of the ritual nature of coming and going, we find:

> Tell the children what kind of behavior you expect at recess time and lunch time. Have them practice routines of lining up in an orderly manner.
> Practice routines for going to gym and fire drill behavior. (Ilnitski, 1974, p. 127)

Opening and closing rituals at the beginning and end of the school day, week, or year are expanded combinations of these entry and activity change rituals. Such entries and exits are marked by ritualized convocations, honors assemblies, registration procedures, and graduation exercises. These are particularly critical times during which group members may be anxious about the roles they are to play, and confusion may reign in the group. The teacher may shape these large or small scale crises through ritual use of time and space from the moment the student enters the school. Once again the "old pro" speaks on how to handle the first day of class.

> Much confusion can be avoided if you have your routine well planned. I would suggest the following:
> Greet children as they enter the room and tell them to take any seat. Encourage them to look through the books, but advise them not to exchange them.
> Have opening exercises.
> Look over your class. Reseat the children. I usually alternate a boy

and a girl, etc. You will be changing their seats many times through-out the school year.[2]

Fill out a seating plan.

If the books are numbered, jot on your index cards the numbers of the books each child has.

Assign lockers and jot down locker numbers.

Have a concrete plan for the day. (Ilnitski, 1974, p. 126)

RITE OR WRONG

Classroom rituals to strengthen the leader status, to promote the common welfare, and to deal with transitional crises have not been exhaustively reviewed here. No doubt others come to the reader's mind from personal experience. We all have spent enough time in schools to have a storehouse of examples, if we are able to stand back and consider school experiences in terms of ritual be-havior. Student-student, student-administrator, teacher-teacher, and teacher-administrator relationships all provide interactions that can be examined for ritual characteristics.

Inevitably the educator will look at such rituals and say, "Yes, that may be the way it *is* now, but is that the way it *should* be?" How does the potential utility balance out with the potential hazards of ritulization, not just at the time of its use, but later in the lives of the group members?

Ritualization can decrease spontaneity and creativity. By locking participants into routine uses of time and space, no room may be left for innovation and discovery. Certainly the extension of ritual to all portions of the school day may have a stultifying effect on creative behavior. It is also true that, while nearly all teachers insist they seek and assist creative behavior, there are some who would just as soon not have to deal with anything disruptive like that in their own classrooms. For them ritualization means safety. It can also mean a safe though boring environment for their students. Students have

---

[2]On what basis have we been fixing and changing students' space? Are we even conscious of why we seat students as we do? Teacher preference? Student requests? What, then, are the long range effects of such spatial manipulation? How do children perceive themselves and others, and how do they behave as a result of years of being fit into a seating chart?

been known to subtly force new teachers, or innovative teachers, to revert to such patterns because of their safety and predictability. There is, after all, comfort in predictability. It is reassuring to know one will always have a designated space and a time when others expect one to be present and perform defined behaviors.

Note, however, that people in our culture whose lives are ritualized to an extreme are considered mentally ill. Such behavior is a commonly described aspect of autism, an obsessive extreme that is not necessarily a product of a too ritualized environment. Extremes aside, there are many in our society who have come to prefer that others structure their daily lives for them and that each day have a ritualized sameness. Such preferences for routinization would seem not only to reduce creative behavior, but to place control of the actions of the many in the hands of those few who have or take the power to instigate and maintain ritualized behavior in others. Those who control where one may be, and when one may be there, can totally order the lives of the group for beneficent or evil purposes. The fictional societies drawn, for example, by George Orwell in *Nineteen Eighty Four* and Ray Bradbury in *Fahrenheit 451* are based on this very premise.

School Rituals Under Fire

In recent years many educators' voices have been raised against the safe nature of the heavily ritualized traditional classroom. The highly routinized, nontransgressable patterns have been blamed for producing adults who are uncreative, unaware, and unthinking in an increasingly authoritarian nation. School critics point to the nonquestioning follow-the-leader thinking as a factor in some of our recent national and international government scandals and trace the sheep-like behavior to classroom training. Authors such as Fromm (1947, 1955) and Goldhammer (1969) decry the automatons that human beings have become.

Toffler (1970) has urged that our society must quickly teach young people not how to fit into what is, as we have been doing, but how to avoid the symptoms of future shock by preparing for what will be. Some critics would do away with everything routine about the traditional public school (Gross & Gross, 1969; Illich, 1970).

On the surface it would appear that the trend in schools has been to do away with ritual—to replace it with totally flexible use of time and space in learning activities directed by student interest rather than teacher specification. In many schools the self-contained classroom, peopled by one teacher and 30 students following a regular schedule, has been phased out. In its place one finds large numbers of children, flexibly grouped, led by any one of a number of teachers, using self-pacing materials, during frequently modified time modules. Such structural reorganizations would appear to abandon prescriptions for the use of time and space in favor of a "do your own thing" arrangement and, indeed, in some schools this has been tried.

Rituals to Maximize Freedom

On closer inspection, however, the successful open classroom depends on the use of ritual just as the self-contained classroom does. It uses ritual to maximize freedom rather than to insure absolute safety and predictability. For the individualized, open classroom to work for the benefit of the students, all persons must be well schooled in the procedures that help them move from area to area and time to time with maximum ease. Nothing can be more chaotic than 80 to 100 students in a large open space with no routines for getting organized upon entry, for leaving, for changing activities, for receiving attention, for group cohesion, or for building respected leadership. I have seen situations where over 100 sixth-, seventh-, and eighth-graders literally ran wild over desks, chairs, and tables in an open pod because regular routines had not been established.

The rituals may differ somewhat in the traditional classroom and the open space pods, particularly in that in the open space some of the rituals are carried out by individuals at their own pace rather than in a group acting in concert. Because student movement and time use is individualized, the controls on participant behavior must more often be internalized than they are in the traditional teacher-dominated environment. Students are called on to demonstrate a higher level of self-discipline. But there are still rituals in both settings that can be observed to build respect for leadership, to smooth social relations in the common interest of the group, and to avoid confusion and anxiety during crises of change.

Some beginning teachers have come to believe in the need for some ritualization in their classrooms, though they may call it by another name. They indicate that, when used in moderation, it allows greater possibilities for students to express themselves and engage in productive learning experiences. One beginning secondary teacher working in an open classroom said:

> There are certain things I deem important—the physical structure, little preliminaries that I have to have taken care of, and then in our disucssions every day it is informal and they can speak out without raising hands. That may be three minutes at the beginning and three at the end, but it ties it in better. If they were bunched in little groups, I think it would be bad for them. But instead they walk in. They know what is expected of them. They sit down. I think the kids, with me, think of that first. It is very important for me to set up that structure. It makes me more comfortable. I feel like I have more control. It is kind of reinforcement to me that I am in comand and things are going OK.

This new teacher had become aware that she consciously manipulated the daily environment by consistently requiring a ritual use of time and space at the beginning and end of the period. The teacher also indicated that these rituals were as important to her peace of mind as they were to the students. If certain procedures were not followed, the teacher's sense of competence was lost. Richardson (1967) spoke critically of just such teacher techniques.

> There is a common assumption about the reassuring effects of a display of administrative efficiency at the beginning of any relationship that has a tutorial function. But it is very much open to question whether the reassurance is for the benefit of the group or for the benefit of the teacher. (p. 25)

However, there appears to be no reason to believe, as Richardson indicates, that actions must exclusively benefit either the teacher or the students. Instead, it seems likely that benefits are derived by all members of the group, teacher included, if the rituals are used in moderation with the goal of promoting responsible freedom.

Know Your Rites

Perhaps, as in so many aspects of life, the rituals of time and space in the hidden curriculum must be judged on their sparing use. Certainly, I hope, it is not the aim of the schools of today to squelch creativity and problem-solving behaviors by over organizing, over-ritualizing the child's use of time and space. Children must be given free time to use the educational space as they choose, for if they never have the opportunity to plan how to use free time and space, how will they ever learn? But it seems equally obvious that if members of a classroom group are not committed to performance of certain rituals that facilitate living together, so much time may be spent in technical and organizational matters that planned curriculum content will receive minimal attention.

One might compare the situation to the routine of brushing one's teeth. On the one hand, if you brush your teeth purely out of habit, you are apt to brush the same way each time and consistently miss certain spots, which may result in trouble over time. At the other extreme, if you have no relatively fixed procedure for toothbrushing you can become so concerned about the technical aspects of brush holding, toothpaste application, and brushing techniques, that you become paralyzed by detail. (Watch a small child learning to brush her or his teeth for the first time if you question this analogy.) At their best, it would seem that a toothbrushing ritual and classroom rituals begin from a relatively fixed pattern on the technical details but include variations and embellishments as new situations arise.

The rituals of the classroom group require planning for stability and flexibility much like that described by Sarason (1972). Speaking of the work of the authors of the U.S. Constitution, he says:

> What is important is that these men began to create a setting. . . not by assuming that shared values were necessary and sufficient for success but by contriving and inventing ways which might protect these values against man's tendencies to act rashly, selfishly, and corruptly; *not by deluding themselves that the end product of their labors was adequate for all time but by specifically providing for change and orderly change which in principle could undo all they had done.* (p. 17; italics mine)

How can teachers, who are so caught up in the events of the classroom, draw back and thoughtfully observe, first, what rituals they actually employ, and then, whether the rituals used in their classrooms are productive of self-disciplined, creative individual and group effort? How can teachers assess the changes needed and lead the group in remodeling the rituals?

Sarason (1972) has defined several processes that occur in all group settings and on which members must be agreed if the goals of the organization are to be met. If these issues are not worked out by the group members, regardless of their shared values, the group will fail. Issues facing the group are as follows:

Anticipation of problems and potential coping procedures

Task distribution and performance

Knowledge and use of resources (time, space, things)

The governing constitution development

Conflict handling methods

Managing foreign relations

Managing numerical growth (p. 12)

While such a list offers no method for analysis of group rituals, consideration of present classroom methods of carrying out each process may help to pinpoint some areas of group behavior that are heavy with ritual processes and others that have no agreed-on procedures at all.

Some questions the teacher might ask about group processes of living together are:

Do we take the time to discuss problems that might arise in regard to classroom members, and have we talked about ways these problems might be handled? For example, what would happen if a member became ill or had a family crisis?

Has a method been established for doing the jobs that need to be done, e.g., who does the housekeeping chores and what are the standards for acceptable work? What penalties and rewards are offered and who controls them?

What understanding has been reached on the use and control of time, space, and resources? Who has access? What procedures must be followed to acquire these?

How are the governing rules established and modified? For example, are regular legislative sessions held? How are they run? When is the teacher's veto power used?

When conflicts or arguments arise, is there a procedure agreed on by the group for ajudication? Is it a teacher-controlled process or a peer-controlled process?

What happens when outsiders enter the group temporarily? If the principal or a parent visits, is a certain procedure followed?

What happens when a new student arrives in class?

As one goes through such questions on the processes of the group, it becomes evident that the rituals developed in response to certain group needs interlock with other rituals. The arrival of a new student may present problems of sharing resources, performing tasks, and conflict management. If a breakdown occurs because procedures are not developed in certain areas of interaction, the negative effects may reach into other areas as well. If, for example, students didn't know what housekeeping chores they were to perform, conflicts could arise over tasks as well as over resources used in housekeeping. These conflicts might mushroom if no resolution method were agreed on.

It may also be noted that all the processes mentioned can be dictated by the teacher or adopted jointly by agreement of all group members. The point of origin of the ritualized procedures would appear to have a great deal to do with the commitment of the group members to appropriate enactment.

Once teachers have identified the rituals functioning in their own hidden curricula, the relevant question becomes, "How much is enough?" Each teacher must make this judgment independently. It is likely that there is no one all-purpose formula, but the optimum will be found to vary with the students, the curriculum content, the environment, and the ultimate goals of the school. It may well be that ritual use will continue to be a somewhat intuitive process, part of the "art" of teaching. An ancient Chinese saying offers the following guidance:

Recognition of law is a first requirement for education. Wisely applied disciplines reveal the seriousness of life as good. But to let discipline degenerate into continuous drill only humiliates a man as the monotony cripples his productive powers. True education awakens within the learner his own intuitive, creative initiative.

It may simply be enough that teachers be made aware of the possible effects of ritual and be urged to review their use of it from time to time. The hidden curriculum may not often rise to the awareness level of the students, but it certainly should not be hidden from the teacher.

Suggested Readings

Adams, Raymond S., & Biddle, Bruce J. *Realities of teaching.* New York: Holt, 1970.

A revealing look at how the teacher manipulates time and space in the classroom and how the classroom environment molds the teacher.

Eliade, Mircea. *The sacred and the profane: The nature of religion.* New York: Harper & Row, 1961.

Includes consideration of the roles of time and space in the religious experiences of humankind.

Goldhammer, Robert. *Clinical supervision.* New York: Holt, 1969.

This is for those who wish to read a scathing attack on the overly ritualized classroom. The first chapter indicts today's schools and teaching methods.

Jackson, Philip. *Life in the classroom.* New York: Holt, 1968.

Jackson writes primarily about what happens in elementary school classrooms. He observed in classrooms and talked with students and teachers over a three-year period to bring together this description of "the elements of repetition, redundancy, and ritualistic action" experienced in the classroom.

Lehmann, C. F. Analyzing and managing the physical setting of the classroom group. In Nelson B. Henry (Ed.), *The dynamics of instructional groups* (The 59th Yearbook of the National Society for the Study of Education, Part II). Chicago: University of Chicago Press, 1960. Pp. 253-267.

Even after a number of years, Lehman's remarks on the effects of physical setting on learning are timely. He questions the adequacy of the average classroom for supporting optimum learning and suggests that intelligent management of adequate physical facilities can multiply teaching-learning possibilities.

Sarason, Seymour B. *The creation of settings and the future societies.* San Francisco: Jossey-Bass, 1972.

Sarason provides many keys to examining groups, settings, and leaders with numerous examples from education.

Snyder, Benson R. *The hidden curriculum.* New York: Knopf, 1971.

A look at how college freshmen learn the hidden curriculum at highly competitive M.I.T. Kindergarteners probably learn the ins and outs of public school the same way.

"Hurry! says the morning,
Don't be late for school!

Hurry! says the teacher,
Hand in papers now!

Hurry! says the mother,
Supper's getting cold!

Hurry! says the father,
Time to go to bed!

Slowly, says the darkness,
You can talk to me . . ."*

*The above piece was spontaneously selected in a poem
reading assignment by one of the author's sixth-grade
students. Is this really the way the world appears to the
young? Are these the predominant messages that reach
them? In this chapter, an experienced teacher explores
space and time in the classroom for the betterment of
school life for all.*

Time and Space in Schools

BEVERLY HARDCASTLE LEWIS**

Time and space are the settings for life, which is indeed our ultimate concern. How can we, as teachers, apply what we have learned
thus far to improve the quality of life in our classrooms and schools
for our students and ourselves? What are the temporal and spatial

---

*From "Hurry" by Eve Merriam. Reprinted from *Out Loud* (New York: Atheneum, 1973) with permission of the author and the publisher.

**The assistance given by Brenda Conlon, State University of New York in Geneseo; Laura Roland, Avon Central School, Avon, New York; and Catherine Ramsey, Geneseo Central School, Geneseo, New York, is gratefully acknowledged here for their thoughtful responses to an earlier version of the manuscript.

conditions of today's classrooms and schools, and how are they shaping and toning school life? If changes are needed, how can we begin?

We may regard the life, space, and time in classrooms from two major viewpoints—the child's and the teacher's. We may turn our heads toward the past, present, or future. Let us begin by looking from a child's viewpoint at the present to see the conditions that exist in today's schools.

THE CHILD'S VIEW

What Children See

The viewpoint conjectured here will be that of a child eight to twelve years old, attending a structurally traditional school in a middle-class community. For other children in other settings there would be differences, but these generally would be differences in degree rather than in kind.

Owned spaces

From the child's viewpoint, which school spaces belong to children? We can note such ownership by observing where children keep their possessions and by noting their use of possessive labels—"my desk," "Shawn's locker," "our classroom." A quick survey of these spaces is offered in Table 1.

Owned time

Time may be more simply discussed, for so little of it can be regarded as belonging to the children. Recess and lunch time may be counted on by children as being theirs. In some classes break time or free time is given for the purpose of visiting and relaxing, and children regard such time with a sense of ownership. Free study periods and project work periods may also be regarded as owned time by children, since they have more control of the use of the time.

Individual space

There are variations in the amount of space a child regards as being personally his or hers. We notice some children in classrooms who use only one section of their desktops to work on, while others spread themselves and their work out onto any neighboring work

Table 1: Child-owned Spaces

Desk:	Probably the most valued and protected space. In very traditional classrooms it may be the child's only source of personal space. In more open classes it may be shared with others or no longer be a part of the school furniture.
Locker:	Often shared with others. Considered a convenience space.
Special Class Seat:	In music, art, or library, if seats are assigned, a certain degree of ownership will be attached to the seat.
Chair:	Often individuals and the group will recognize individual ownership of chairs. Robert Sommer (1969) notes: "People who remain in public areas for long periods—whether at a habitual chair at a weekly conference or on a commuter train—can establish a form of tenure. Their rights to this space will be supported by their neighbors even when they are not physically present." (p. 52)
Boys' or Girls' Bathroom:	Definitely a child's space and not a teacher's. A private retreat for tears, anger, fights, secrets, mischief and day dreams. In some schools it becomes the communal news center for the underground student communication network. In some secondary schools it may become the property of a group of students or it may be locked by the administration.
Playground:	Child-owned and shared with other children. Powerfully real and memorable considering the relatively limited time spent in recess.
Hall:	A no-man's-land in most schools. A public avenue. Perhaps the sense of ownership would be similar to that felt for one's lane or street at home. In secondary school, the hub of socializing.
Classroom:	A wide range of possible feeling here. In some rooms children feel a sense of ownership for the whole room or sections of it. In other rooms the desk may be the only owned space.
School Building:	Feelings of ownership increase with the years spent in the building. Variations in intensity also depend upon school philosophies, building dimensions, and the degree to which children participate in school activities.

surface—another child's desk, a bookcase, the window ledge. When given choices, some children prefer to move their desks away from the desks of others. "I work better this way," they say or, "I don't like being all bunched up." Some choose to be close to others, with desks touching side-by-side or opposite each other. Needs vary from person to person, and an individual's needs vary from day to day.

Sommer (1969) refers to this individual space ownership as "personal space," and Hall relates such spaces to "spatial envelopes" (1969). This personal life space is further described as:

> the emotionally charged zone around each person, sometimes described as a soap bubble or aura, which helps to regulate the spacing of individuals. (Sommer, 1969, p. viii)

The limits of personal space become evident through interaction with either the environment or other people. The desk location preferences discussed above indicate some of the limits. Other cues come from the selection of the length of distance separating individuals who are interacting. If the distance is short, the interaction is likely to be intimate and informal; if the distance is great, the interaction will probably be more reserved and formal.

So when we regard a classroom in spatial terms, we may learn much by noticing the physical distances separating people. Variations in these physical distances are due to a number of influences: "the cultural background, the relationship of the interactants, the topic being discussed, and the personal and attitudinal characteristics of the two parties" (Knapp, 1971, p. 244). The sex of the people relating is another significant influence. We may be further helped in our efforts to find meaning in personal spaces by Hall's (1969) designation of four areas of spatial actions. He defines these in terms of the nature of the situation and transaction: *intimate* distance is from contact to about 18 inches; *personal* distance is from 18 inches to perhaps 4 feet; *social* distance is from 4 to maybe 12 feet; and *public* distance is from 12 to 25 feet or more (pp. 116-125).

The selection of spatial distance communicates in classrooms, as elsewhere. The teacher who stands before his or her class most of the time is discouraging interaction with those who sit at the back of the class (and vice versa) for, "It is difficult to have an intimate conversation with someone who is 30 feet away" (Adams and Biddle, 1970, p. 89). The teacher who sits beside a child communicates support or interest even without a verbal message. The unspoken power of such spatial language is illustrated by an incident related by Koch (1971):

> We asked one teacher to deliberately try moving closer to students when they were working in small groups at tables. She reported that it was very hard to do. She felt conspicuous and ill at ease, and so uncomfortable that she would have given up on further attempts had she not gotten immediate, positive feedback from her students. They sent her messages thay they liked the warmth and interest that her closer proximity engendered. In a short time, drawing near to students became a natural act for her. (p. 232)

A second teacher tried a similar experiment, and Koch notes that it was unsuccessful because the movement was so counter to the teacher's natural inclination. The children responded to other non-verbal cues and read the movement as insincere.

In sensing their own individual space and in interpreting that of others, children in classrooms participate in a subtle but powerful language that psychologists and sociologists are still trying to decipher. Of significance to teachers in terms of nonverbal communications and spatial language is the finding that when verbal and nonverbal communication signals conflict, "We turn to nonverbal, whether we realize it or not, for verification" (Koch, 1971, p. 232).

Individual time

The influence of developmental psychologists, including Piaget's sequential stages of cognitive growth, is being felt in the classrooms. Teachers are accepting and adapting to the varying rates in which individuals grow. For the beginning teacher, individual time variations must be among the first classroom challenges. Each child has his or her own time table and growth rate, and the sooner the teacher realizes this and acts upon it, the better life will be for both the students and the teacher.

Collective time

It is helpful to note the distinctions between individual and collective times in schools. Individuals have natural time senses tuned to their personal moods, energies, and inclinations. Often in conflict with these is collective time. The classroom group will have its own collective moods, desires, and needs, which overcome individual needs whenever they are in conflict. In group planning sessions, selection of recess games, and seating arrangement choices, individuals may have to give up their desires for the group's decision.

Clock time

To instruct a large number of students with a smaller number of teachers, time needs to be apportioned. Students, teachers, and administrators must give up personal preferences to meet the requirements of physical or clock time. The student who wishes to finish an art project must give in to the clock time that designates the end of the art period, for another class will begin, and the art place will be taken by another student. The teacher who wishes to spend a few more minutes discussing a section of a film must move along quickly for lunch period is coming up. The administrator who wishes to speak to whole faculty privately must schedule the meeting before or after school hours. Clock time is a reality in every part of life and at every age, so school clock time should not appear to be so oppressive. It is, however, helpful for teachers to be aware of the collective and clock time limits placed on individuals, for they may then be more considerate in placing further time limits on students. Students who wish to daydream during a free reading period should perhaps be allowed to respond to their individual time senses and do so.

Calendar time

It is most helpful for teachers to be aware of the subtle but often blatant influence of calendar time in schools. Changes in attitudes among students—and teachers—are predictably related to calendar time. Changes occur at the end of the year, on days before vacations, and to a lesser extent on Fridays. No one has coined a word for this phenomenon, though "school fatigue," "seeing-the-stable-door," or "psychic-switch" might apply. Stebbins (1974) refers to it in this way:

> Mental fatigue is probably a less significant factor in the burgeoning unquiet and disorderliness that heralds the approach of these occasions than anticipation by the students of activities they will engage in while away from the classroom. (p. 55)

Test manufacturers recognize the phenomenon when they advise that their tests not be given on Fridays, Mondays, and days immediately preceding or following vacations.

The calendar time of our schools is marked off in such a way that we can predict periods of student restlessness and low motivation with relative ease. If we wish to initiate activities or experiences that will demand student commitment, academic energy, and time duration, it is best to avoid these predictable points. Further, in our plans for Friday afternoons, pre-vacation days, and end of the year weeks, we might either try to compete with the out-of-school lure by designing especially enjoyable lessons or attempt to integrate the class's sense of restlessness and anticipation into lessons in some meaningful way.

CHILD'S VIEWPOINT: DREAM SCHOOLS

How would children prefer to see time and space used in schools? To learn how some children felt, I gave my sixth-grade class an optional creative writing assignment with the directive: "Describe a school that would use time and space in better ways than we see in today's schools." Earlier in the year the children had described their ideal schools in another writing assignment. In these papers the writers' thoughts seemed to center on curricula, lunch, snacks, recess, gym classes, and classroom gadgets. In this second assignment the children were asked to focus on time and space only and to keep in mind the purposes of school. The purposes were left undefined, and no interpretations of "better ways" were suggested.

The assignment was given during the last two weeks of school, and in accordance with the calendar time phenomenon discussed above, it was playfully offered as bait to the imaginative. Those who did not want to write on the subject could write on other suggested topics or read a book of their own choosing. No deadline was given and as the assignments were completed and handed in, they were read to the class, commented on by the teacher, revised or corrected, and then finally returned to the teacher.

Four of the papers are included here as a sample. Of interest to me are the ideas the children suggest and the assumptions they presume. Further, by considering the negatives or polarities of their statements and by noting what they choose to omit, we may grasp their concepts of life, space, and time in existing classrooms. Through their dreams, we glimpse reality.

(Untitled) by Debbie M.

The schools are one story above ground and two below ground. Stairs going up and down or go down on slides.

Go to school from 8:00 A.M. to 12:00 noon. Study all the subjects you can in that time period. One day a week have all free sports. You can do any sport you want that there is an instructor for. You have one hour per sport. Go Monday through Friday.

The top level has one room off the rest of building with all glass, and ground floor with dirt and grass. Trees and foliage growing and a few animals, too. The room is huge. That is a wildlife class. You go once a week. Only 12 kids per class go there. Feed the animals and learn how to take care of them and help them if they are hurt. Learn which plants are poisonous and non-poisonous.

At end of school year the class goes on a weekend camping trip.

The School "My Way" by Lisa M.

Space: I opened the door. The baby-blue board was on my left. My bed on my right. In front of me was the kitchen, and cupboards and stove and refrigerator. (See Figure 1)

Time: As I walked into the apartments, I took the elevator up to the eighth floor where my room was. You see all us kids had rooms with maid service. My room was pink with purple polka dots. We had telephones to call for pizza or whatever we wanted. We had a special screen (like a tv) that at every odd hour we would turn on (every odd hour between 8:00 and 2:00) and have our class lessons. Then after our 30 minute lesson we had 30 minutes free time or to do any homework. For homework we wrote on a blackboard. Everyone had a different color blackboard. Mine was baby-blue with pink chalk! We would do our homework on it, then push a button and it was corrected.

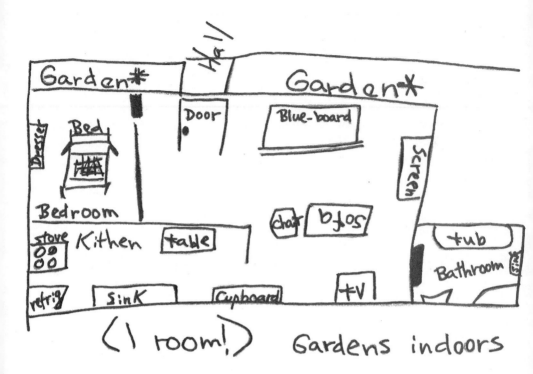

Figure 1: Lisa's Space

Schools!!! by Mary Beth M.

If I had a choice of how to form a school, I would only go to school Monday, Wednesday and Friday. And have it like you go to math class, then you can come home and do whatever you want, then go to a different class like college. Then I would have an elevator to get to your classes instead of walking up ten flights of stairs, and everybody would get to use it.

Then go to school 8:00 in the morning until 2:30 in the afternoon.

Then if you get suspended from school have it two days instead of three so your mom and dad don't kill you as much. When you get into 7th grade you can have 45 minutes to go horse back riding if you want, like on trails and in the woods and wherever you want as long as you're on school grounds and have a teacher along with you. Then when you get back from horse back riding you clean the saddles and brush the horse. . . . . (Here she knowledgeably describes the procedure and materials for horse grooming.) Then when you get done doing that, go back to work. If some of the boys would rather play football then let them just have a gym teacher out there to watch them.

And only have one math period.

(Untitled) by Tim A.

One day I was walking down along the wood and came upon a beautiful white mare, with her newborn fillie. I stood and looked at the two. I looked at the sun. It was twelve o'clock. I had to run to make it home in time for dinner. I ran and tripped in a wood chuck hole and sprained my ankle.

I fell into a deep sleep and dreamed all the schools closed and our parents taught us what we knew. Ouch. The white mare bit me on the nose. Now I was not late for dinner. I was late for school!

Interpreting the Dreams

I would like to use an analysis of these children's papers as a paradigm for the analysis of school space and time in a larger context. What we are concerned with are children and teachers, and time and space, all within a school context. We thus have a field or a network to study, and when we examine any one part of it, we gain insight into all others.

Temporal and spatial boundaries

In the four students' papers the school boundaries are less rigid than those found in today's schools. Home and school, outdoors and indoors, mix more freely. Tim would have home and nature replace school. Debbie suggests an all-glass room, which would give the illusion of being outdoors. Her school also contains the outdoors in a below-ground-level wildlife classroom complete with trees and foliage. Lisa's school resembles a high-rise apartment building with home-like conveniences, kitchens, bathrooms, bedrooms, and gardens. In Mary Beth's school the physical boundary is broken by breaks in the time boundary as students move back and forth between home and school frequently. Her class meetings would be scheduled more like college ones, and school days would alternate with home days. She would also have horseback riding times "on trails and in the woods and wherever you want as long as you're on school grounds."

Other educators have observed similar desires for the removal of boundaries. In Coles's article, "Those Places They Call Schools" (1969), children speak in angrier tones:

> And once you're inside, you never see the outside until the big bell rings and you can leave, if the teacher says yes, it's o.k. . . .If they put on the radio, like we have at home, it would be better than not hearing anything but yourself and the clock. (p. 52)

Two other children whom Coles quotes in the article describe a school that they would like with "a window in the roof so you could just look up and see the sky and the clouds and the sun and when the rain falls you could see it falling and you'd like it better, being in school" (p. 51).

Teachers, too, express their frustrations at being bound by the school environment. Sarason (1971) met with young high school teachers weekly for a year to discuss any problems they were having. Near the end of the year he noted, "They complained that their days were not varied, school was a well-insulated fortress, and that they felt locked into a system that has some characteristics of a factory" (p. 166).

More extreme reactions to boundaries can be found in ghetto schools, for there the boundaries are not merely isolating and unnatural, they are openly hostile and pervasive. A welfare mother commented:

> The schools are like jails. The classrooms are locked. When the kids are inside, they are locked for "safety." When the kids are outside, they are locked so nobody can steal anything. There are iron gates in the hallway. (Sommer, 1974, p. 83)

The locked boundaries extend to the ghetto or stem from it so that simply rebuilding a school or opening locked classrooms will not solve the problems. As one ghetto youth said:

The rat that bit my kid sister, he's not going to stop and say, "Well, well, what a nice school, I think I'll stay clear of it." (Coles, 1969, p. 56)

Crowding

In the dream schools of the four young writers we can interpret a reaction to the crowdedness of classrooms today. Tim places himself outside the school in an unconfined setting. Debbie describes her wildlife room as "huge" and "only 12 kids per class go there." For Debbie school expands even more at the end of the year when "the class goes on a weekend camping trip." In Mary Beth's school children are allowed to ride on trails through the woods. Lisa's apartment size facilities for each student contrast markedly with allotted individual space in present classrooms.

Classroom crowding is incisively examined by Jackson in his book *Life in Classrooms* (1968). Though he was writing about the crowded conditions of the 1960s, much of what he wrote then still applies now. The number of open-space schools has increased dramatically in this country, and walls have been knocked down to open up space in many older schools, but the majority of the schools today are physically the same as they were when Jackson wrote. The self-contained classroom with four walls, housing 25 to 30 students, remains the rule rather than the exception. Jackson's comments are thus still relevant and worth considering.

He discusses the actual physical crowding and the publicness of classrooms, as well as the consequences or by-products of crowding, namely, delays, denial of desires, interruptions, and social distractions. When examined the actual physical crowding is rather startling:

> Even factory workers are not clustered as close together as students in a standard classroom . . . . Only in schools do thirty or more people spend several hours each day literally side by side. (p. 8)

When desks are arranged in rows, as they often are, the sense of crowding is at its greatest.

Time and space become public because of crowding. Grades and teacher's comments on student papers are hard to hide. A student's progress through the test booklet is easily detected by others. Errors in pronunciations in reading groups can be heard by all. Erasures in math or language exercises are noted by neighbors. Indeed:

> Most of the things that are done in school are done with others, or at least in the presence of others, and this fact has profound implications for determining the quality of a student's life. (p. 8)

In the open-space schools life may be even more public because of the increased visual space and thus increased audience size.

One by-product of crowding is delay. When there are many, some personal needs must take second place to group needs. Children must wait in line to go to special classes; they must wait in line to go to lunch; sometimes there are lines for the bathroom, drinks, recess, dismissal, assemblies, and fire drills. In the mornings there are waiting periods while attendance is taken, money collected, or permission slips gathered. When there are not enough school books, supplies, or sports equipment, more waiting ensues.

With the waiting, frustration mounts. Children sit by the classroom door so that they'll be first in line. They rush across the classroom to get the encyclopedia they need. They place a premium on low batting orders on the playground. For often if they are not first, or among the first, they lose out completely. Recess is over before the sixth batter's turn. All of the E volumes of encyclopedias are being used. The cafeteria just ran out of pizza. Small matters, certainly, but they help explain why children who normally walk at home run at school.

Some of the delays may be eliminated through better planning and organization. Children, if they are responsible enough, may "sign out" of the classroom for their trips to the bathroom, drinking fountain, or library by noting on the blackboard their name and destination. Teachers may schedule lengthy multi-disciplinary work periods so that books and supplies will not be in demand by all at the same time. Recess periods may be extended by the teacher until everyone has a turn or the game is finished.

However, not all delays can be eliminated. These may be regarded instrumentally as opportunities for children to learn how to use free moments. If children are made aware of ways that they can use these "time vacuums"—reading, sketching, conversing, observing, imagining, thinking—they may find school time less frustrating, and the frequent delays in the out-of-school world will become easier to manage.

Another by-product of crowding is the denial of desires. The small denials of pizza and turns at batting were noted above. Deeper denials occur when a child wishes to relate a personal feeling or experience to a friend, the teacher, or the class and there is not enough time. It may be noon before a teacher or the class learn about the death of a favorite pet or the vacation to Florida, because the opportunities for talk were limited or too many people had something to say.

A third by-product of crowding is interruption. Jackson writes of this:

> During group sessions irrelevant comments, misbehavior, and outside visitors bearing messages often disrupt the continuity of the lesson. When the teacher is working individually with a student ... petty interruptions, usually in the form of other students coming to the teacher for advice, are the rule rather than the exception. (pp. 15-17)

Time thus can become fragmented by the crowding of space. Teachers and their students may work together to seek solutions for this problem.

The final by-product of crowding that Jackson notes is social distractions. The close proximity of others in the same room makes it difficult to concentrate on independent work. Looks, whispers, note-passing, signals—all vie for the student's attention, while the teacher discourages or outlaws communication. "These young people, if they are to become successful students, must learn how to be alone in a crowd" (Jackson, 1968, p. 16). There are ways to work on this problem, however, again through joint efforts. One student in my class suggested that our mornings be spent for silent independent work and afternoons be spent on non-silent group work. She further suggested that we arrange the desks into "test-taking formation"—spread out so that all desks are apart—in the morning and form large desk groups in the afternoon. We tried this, and it was quite successful in combating three of Jackson's by-products: delays, interruptions, and social distractions.

Architects and builders do consider the amount of space provided in terms of the number of people to be housed. However, there are discrepancies between what is recommended and what is practiced. Lehmann (1960) writes:

> Square-foot-per-pupil ratios have a deceptive way of solidifying into prescriptive standards. Particularly does this seem to be true of "recommended minimums" which often become performance norms and maximums. (p. 254)

Lehmann further notes the need to be concerned with the sonic environment of classrooms:

> Undue noise is fatiguing, in the classroom or anywhere. Although the children in the class may adjust to it, they do so at some cost in expenditure of energy. (p. 254)

Twenty-five or 30 people speaking in normal voices in an average-sized classroom can make a considerable amount of noise. Indoor recess periods with children playing board games, jacks, blackboard games, or just talking may be physically draining on teachers and children purely because of noise strain. This may be a reason that mum ball is such a popular recess game. Noise is forbidden in this game of catch. If someone groans or speaks out, he or she is immediately out of the game. Another popular recess game, 7-Up, is also silent. In this game seven children walk around the room while others in the class sit at their desks with their heads down. The seven touch seven seated people, and the children touched guess the identity of those who touched them. The silent nature of each game, while not a primary cause of enjoyment, may well be a secondary one.

Creating new spaces

One obvious but expensive solution to the problem of crowding would be the construction of open-space schools. In these, additional space is created by eliminating halls and walls. In traditionally built schools walls may be knocked down or wings added. However, if these structural changes are too costly, much still can be done by using the existing space in better ways. Drummond's article, "Using Time, Space, and Things Creatively" (1975), is an excellent source of practical ideas toward this end. He suggests that stages, closets, dressing rooms, and cafeterias be used for tutoring and individual work; that a tent or cardboard box be used in a classroom as a place for individual retreat or small group work; and that halls become science centers, listening posts, miniature city halls, or places for individual study equipped with fold-out tables and storage units. Drummond offers close to 50 suggestions for creating new spaces from the existing space. In addition, he jars us into seeing our surroundings in new ways.

Teacher use of classroom space is examined by Maxson in her article, "Toward Understanding the Use and Impact of Teaching Space" (1975). She notes:

> Classroom life centers around activities involving books, desks, chairs, and possibly tables, and other classroom artifacts. Because environment places constraints upon people, the arrangement of these environmental "props," to a large extent, extablishes not only the amount of flow and movement possible within the classroom, but also the type of activities that are likely to take place. (p. 179)

Maxson stresses the need for awareness and further study of this dimension of classroom life and space. By being aware of their present use of classroom space and by being creative in their search for solutions, teachers may indeed create new spaces within the old.

Authority's spatial and temporal limits

When we look back at the four student papers, we notice a somewhat startling absence. In none is a teacher or an authoritative role described. This may be accounted for by the fact that the papers were written for a teacher, and perhaps the children assumed a teacher would be included in the environment and need not be mentioned. I feel, however, that the absence is significant. Space and time in schools are defined and limited most often by authority figures. Children see spatial limits set by the principal, "Do not leave the school grounds," "Sit with your class for the assembly," and "Stay out of the gym after dismissal." They report to the principal's office when they are tardy and take their excuses there after they have been absent and thus associate the principal with temporal limits. Principals vary in the softness or harshness with which they set the limits, but to be responsible for the children's safety and education, they must set limits. Similarly teachers set limits for their classes spatially: "Stay in your seats," "Line up," "Do not leave the room without my permission," "Walk on the right side of the hall," "Do not leave the lunchroom until I come for you." And they set temporal limits: "Let us say the pledge," "You have 50 minutes for this test," "Your homework is due Thursday," and "When we're all ready, we will go." Some teachers are stricter than others, but in the end even the most lenient must set limits for safety's sake, if nothing else.

Why then have these figures been excluded from the "Dream Schools?" Tim eliminates school authority completely in his paper. Lisa's teacher is a minimally interfering authority, appearing on a television screen at every odd hour for 30 minutes. Debbie mentions a gym teacher: "You can do any sport you want that there is an instructor for." Mary Beth does the same: "horse back riding . . . wherever you want as long as . . . and have a teacher along with you," and "Then if some of the boys would rather play football then let them, just have a gym teacher out there to watch them." It is relevant to note that during the year in a neighboring school, a child was paralyzed as a result of an injury that occurred during a gym class. Children could see the potential for tragedy in gym classes as a result of this sad experience, and this may be why my writers were careful to include a teacher in their sports settings. In all other settings teachers are absent.

Perhaps the children would rather not have a teacher present in the other school settings. Perhaps they resist the limits on their space and time.

Finally we may view the children's dream schools as unconscious expressions of sexual differences in perceptions of school time and school space. It is poignant that Tim's ideal school is no school. This attitude is held by more boys than girls. That boys find school more uncomfortable than girls do can be documented statistically and by noting that more boys drop out of school, repeat grades, have reading problems, have stuttering difficulties, require more disciplining, complain about school more, and have lower marks (Peltier, 1968, p. 182).

The freedom sensed in Tim's dream is checked in the girls' dreams. This may be a reflection of sex role traits that society consciously and unconsciously assigns to boys and girls. Boys are supposed to be freer and more adventurous, and girls are supposed to be more orderly and obedient. The girls' dreams include schedules, routines, goals, requirements, and limitations. In contrast with their "8:00 Monday, Wednesday, and Friday" types of time structuring,

Tim looks at the sun and says that it is 12 o'clock, dinner time. His view seems freer, more tuned to nature.

Spatially the schools described range from the specifically defined—and thus limited—buildings of Lisa and Debbie, to the slightly broader college type campus of Mary Beth, to Tim's undefined, unlimited open outdoors with woods and woodchuck holes. The differences here may reflect a finding of one recent study that boys are more confident with space and its use and are more comfortable in it than are girls (Saegert and Hart, in press).

Finally it is significant that three of the four dream school papers selected for this discussion were written by girls. More girls completed the assignment, which was optional, and the girls' assignments contained more information than those of the boys. Girls have been generally found to have a greater verbal ability than boys (Maccoby and Jacklin, 1974).

The dream schools have allowed us to see some of the child's view. Now let us turn to the teacher's perspective.

TEACHERS' DILEMMA: THE CHINESE PUZZLE BOX

When examining the authoritative limits placed on children by their teachers, we see that these lie within the limits placed on teachers by principals, and these lie within the limits placed on principals by school boards, and these lie within the limits placed on school boards by society. Hence the Chinese puzzle box, from the inside out.

Defining Limits

Jackson startles us when he refers to teachers as children's first bosses and as prison guards (1968, p. 31). However, have we not heard children say the same? Ask a boy to role-play a teacher, and he will immediately begin giving others orders and directions. Ask a young girl why she wants to be a teacher, and she's likely to reply, "Because I'd get to boss people around."

The limits on children's use of space and time may be set forth directly by the teacher during the first days of school, or they may emerge somewhat mysteriously over the first weeks of school. When they are complete, they can be regarded as a sort of classroom constitution, the working rules of the classroom. Sarason studied the development of such constitutions as they were formed during the first month of school in six suburban middle-grade classrooms. His findings are summarized in Table 2.

Sarason continues by listing the assumptions he feels lie behind the findings, and the reader may wish to examine these in Table 3. At first glance, the list seems to be a reasonable one. A second look, however, shows the assumptions that lie behind these assumptions—namely, that teachers view themselves as being superior and children as being inferior, undemanding, and incompetent. Granted that some teachers may be power hungry, patronizing to children, and insensitive to their needs, most are not. Indeed most teachers have such an appreciation of children—their abilities, needs, and worlds—that they tend to inflate even children's physical size to adult proportions so that upon seeing a child in a non-school setting teachers are startled by the actual smallness of their students.

That teachers are dominant in the formation of classroom constitutions may be the case, but their reasons for this may be viewed less harshly. One assumption that could be added to Sarason's list in

Table 2: Characteristics of Classroom Constitutions

1. The constitution was invariably determined by the teacher. No teacher ever discussed why a constitution was necessary.

2. The teacher never solicited the opinions and feelings of any pupil about a constitutional question.

3. In three of the classrooms the rules of the game were verbalized by the end of the first week of school. In two others the rules were clear by the end of the month. In one it was never clear what the constitution was.

4. Except for the one chaotic classroom, neither children nor teachers evidenced any discomfort with the content of constitutions—it was as if everyone agreed that this is the way things are and should be.

5. In all instances constitutional issues involved what children could or could not, should or should not do. The issue of what a *teacher* could or could not, should or should not do, never arose.

(From Sarason, 1971, p. 176.)

Table 3 is that it is more efficient and orderly for the teacher to define the constitutional terms. Teachers engage in approximately "200 or 300 interpersonal interchanges every hour" (Jackson, 1968, p. 149), and it is understandable that they would seek quick, efficient methods to arrive at a system of order. At the beginning of the year when children are adjusting to the demands placed on them by group life—as well as the academic demands—they lean especially heavily on the teacher as a guide: "Can I get a drink?" "May I go to the bathroom now?" "Betty's kicking my chair;" or "May I sit by Mike?" With each answer the teacher consciously or unconsciously defines the terms of the classroom constitution and limits the use of space and time. It is a matter of meeting small needs quickly and unobtrusively.

A second assumption to add to Sarason's list would be that no one pushed for a change. A certain amount of inertia must be overcome to bring about any change in habit, and unless students, teacher, or both energetically seek the change, the status quo will remain. Apparently no one was unhappy or evidenced discomfort with the situ-

Table 3: Assumptions Offered by Sarason for His Constitutional Issues Study Findings (Table 2)

1. Teacher knows best.
2. Children cannot participate constructively in the development of a classroom constitution.
3. Children want and expect the teacher to determine the rules of the game.
4. Children are not interested in constitutional issues.
5. Children should be governed by what a teacher thinks is right or wrong.
6. The ethics of adults are obviously different from and superior to the ethics of children.
7. Children should not be given responsibility for something they cannot handle or for which they are not accountable.
8. If constitutional issues were handled differently, chaos might result.

(From Sarason, 1971, p. 176)

ation (see no. 4 in Table 2). With many other demands pressing and no one driving for a change, why would time be spent discussing a set of governing rules?

A final assumption to add would be that certain conditions of group life call for the setting of terms by an authority. As two of my student writers noted in their papers, instructors are needed in physical education settings. Gump's study (1964) of counselor interventions in three different camp settings reveals that there are demands inherent in the activity structure itself. Indeed he notes, "Logically, we could ask what the class does to the teacher as readily as we might ask what the teacher does to the class" (p. 181).

With these assumptions in mind, we may better understand why teachers dominate the formation of classroom constitutions; however, we may still find the outcome offensive. Should teachers authoritatively limit children's space and time? What are the alternatives? How can teachers and their students join together to form classroom constitutions? How can they find valid solutions to the problems created by living in a crowd? Once the questions are posed, answers will be found. Children may offer the most creative answers.

Principal's Influence

The authority of principals shapes and tones the spaces in which they and their teachers live. The tone of this authority is echoed often in the classroom by a corresponding teacher-to-pupil authority relationship. If the principal is strict with the faculty, the faculty is likely to be strict with their classes. If the principal is supportive of the faculty and encourages individualistic teaching, a similar attitude may well carry through to the teachers' regard for their pupils.

Principals have it within their power to demoralize faculties and students by rigidly structuring school time and space. Teachers may be required to punch time clocks. Students may be required to have hall passes. Relationships are depersonalized, and the overall quality of life in the school is lowered.

Principals who appreciate the temporal and spatial needs of their teachers are much more likely to promote positive, valuable working relationships between themselves and their teachers. The importance of this is greater than most people think. Teachers are more generous with their time, more supportive of their principals and pupils, and more committed to their schools when such relationships exist. Their positive attitudes extend to the life-space and time in their classrooms.

Society's Influence

Continuing out in the Chinese puzzle box, two more boxes, the school board and society at large, are encountered. The school board box has transparent sides because it acts as a vehicle for the exchange of views between schools—teachers and principals—and society—parents and taxpayers. The box for society is the largest one for our immediate purposes and the most firmly constructed.

In a very real way this last box shapes the limits on teachers and their classes. Society's views on the purpose and value of education will be reflected in its support or lack of support for schools financially and spiritually. Teachers may find options limited by overcrowded classrooms, lack of supplies, rigid curricular guides, and strict accountability requirements. On the other hand, teachers may find their roles to be expansive ones with small classes, abundant supplies, curricular autonomy, and enthusiastic support for innovative methods and programs. These extremes in both directions are rare, but what a teacher will find cannot be predicted.

Society's own time sense affects its regard for schools and educational programs. With Sputnik in the 1950s, the public looked to the future and supported education as an investment. In the 1960s the time focus shifted more to the present, with the immediate problem of Vietnam and the tense energy of the New Frontiers, civil rights movements, and the Great Society. Talented teachers and observers of children were writing about what *is* in classrooms (Ashton-Warner, 1963; Holt, 1964; Kohl, 1967; Marshall, 1963; Moustakas, 1966; and others). The public may have been moved by their writings to improve the "present" conditions of classrooms. It is too soon for assessments concerning the 1970s, but I hypothesize that they will be regarded as a time of distrust and disappointment in both the present and the future. The "ends-justifies-the-means" morality and the polluting, draining, economically confounding technology combine to make a return to the past appealing. Calvinistic austerity budgets cast schools to a past stature. These are all sweeping statements, which are admittedly speculative and generalized. What is of importance, however, is that society's time sense and its regard for schools mark the outer limits of school time and space.

Now that we have come to the last box, which contains all the others, we can see how small and lost that original box is. And what does it contain? Children. Their natural freedom in time and space is indeed boxed in when they come to school—limited by teachers, principals, school boards, and society. We should not forget this. Our limits on their freedoms should not be made capriciously, unthinkingly; instead each limit should have validity in *their* terms, for children are our schools' centers.

FILTERS ON ACTION

As teachers, the images we have of children, the concepts we have of the learning process, our educational philosophies, our personal styles, and the quality of our lives all act as filters on the way we behave in our schools and classrooms. As we limit, define, or enrich the time and space of children, we do so through these filters. By examining these, then, we can better understand how we presently behave and how we wish to change.

Time Values

Do we value the present, future, or past? Are we tuned to children's time orientations? Which time tense predominates in our classrooms?

If we are oriented to the past, we carry on school practices because "things have always been done this way." We continue rituals because "they're traditional." We teach history because it is a "school subject." We begin our astronomy unit because "it's January already." We teach last year's lessons to this year's class.

If we have a future orientation, we regard today as a preparation for tomorrow. We frequently make references to the future. "You must learn to add this year so that you'll be able to multiply next year." "If you can't manage homework now, what are you going to do in high school?" "If you expect to go to college, you'll have to be able to do better than this." Today's pleasures are sacrificed to tomorrow's challenges.

Those who have a present orientation teach more responsively. "The children have been so involved that we may stay on this unit all spring;" "No, I don't have plans for tomorrow. We'll see what happens;" "I'm not giving spelling tests anymore because the children don't enjoy them;" or, "I felt like getting outside so we took a walk."

Jackson (1970) values both present and future orientations in school and suggests the somewhat confusing labels "preparatory" and "consummatory" for these perspectives on education. He considers the official purpose of school to be preparatory, but he notes that it also must be consummatory because "school accounts for so large a portion of human existence" (p. 14). Interestingly, when we recall our own school days, our recollections consist of life moments, not preparations. As a matter of fact, most of our memories take place in the child-owned times and spaces described earlier.

The selection of a single time tense is actually not necessary. All may be integrated into our school time with emphasis on shifting among the three according to the group's nature and needs. It is helpful, however, for teachers to be aware of the workings of these time orientations and to avoid stagnating themselves in only one frame.

When we look to children, our centers of school, we notice that they tend to stress the present. A two-year-old tends to punctuate his or her speech with "now": "I go to Suzanne's now;" "Eat lunch now." Elementary students are inclined to write in the present tense or slip into it when they become involved in their writing:

> The man got off the bus. He said, "What time is it?" I said, "I don't know." He pulled out a gun and ran. He is running toward me. I see his eyes.

In the absence of a secure future, many children gain value only in the present time tense. Even with children who have apparently secure lives, the swaying is to the present. Given choices such as, "Do you want the class party to be tomorrow, next week when we have more time, or would you rather squeeze in something this afternoon?," the typical response will be, "This afternoon!" Those are middle-class elementary children. Meanwhile, Poussaint (1974) writes of the need for immediacy in deprived children:

> Delayed rewards are weak motivators of behavior, as they are discriminatorily and inconsistently given. The more immediate and direct the reward is, the stronger a motivator is likely to be. The future is too far away and too unpredictable. (p. 96)

And, of course, tomorrow seems farther away the younger one is.

Children like immediate feedback. "Read my story," they say as they put down their pencils. "Have you checked my test yet?" they ask minutes after papers have been collected. It may be recalled that Lisa had a dream school equipped with magic blackboards that corrected schoolwork with the push of a button.

The workings of a future orientation have nevertheless brought rewards for children. Singer (1974) writes of a child's "future-focused role image" (p. 32) and notes that the farther children can see into their own futures, the more motivated they are to accept the discomforts of the present as a means to the rewards of the future.

While we become aware of our own time orientations, we do so in a dynamic relationship with the time orientations of children in our classrooms. The power of Singer's future-focused role image is great. If a child believes that some day he or she will be a veterinarian, the memory work of zoology becomes real rather than tedious. Mathematics becomes more tolerable to the future space scientist. The encouragement or discouragement of such future projections lies within the powers of teachers. The cancellation of such a dream is poignantly told by Malcolm X, when he recalled his days of being one of the top students in a predominantly white school. His English teacher asked him what he planned for as a career. Malcom X told the teacher that he was considering becoming a lawyer. His teacher's response was:

> Malcolm, one of life's first needs is for us to be realistic. Don't misunderstand me now. We all here like you, you know that. But you've got to be realistic about being a nigger. A lawyer—that's no realistic goal for a nigger. You need to think about something you *can* be. You're good with your hands—making things. Everybody admires your carpentry shop work. Why don't you plan on carpentry? (X and Haley, 1964, p. 36)

Malcolm added in his autobiography, "It was then that I began to change—inside" (p. 36).

Our view of time as teachers and our view of the time of our students can have a significant effect on the lives of children. It is for this reason that it is best to put aside cumulative folders at the beginning of the year—after gleaning from them only the essential medical and familial facts—for our expectations may be projected to the children nonverbally if not verbally, placing our limits on them. The comments and views of other teachers should be read after a relationship has been established freshly between teacher and student. The teacher should not define the limits of a child's growth.

Images of Learning and Learners

Other conceptualizations, other filters, influence the way teachers act with children. Among these are our images of the learner and of the learning process. For some, students are regarded as unorganized raw materials that teachers transform into acceptable products—the good citizen, the neat worker, the sound thinker. Similar views of the learner have been pejoratively described as "the clean slate" (Yamamoto, 1975, p. 107) and "the empty learner" (Getzels, 1975, p. 3). The industrial and engineering terminology now popular in colleges of education promotes such a view: "observable behavioral objectives," "competency-based teacher education," "performance contracting," "input and output," and "sequential skill programs." These terms may denote useful approaches, but they connote product rather than people orientations.

Further, as Calitri (1975) observes:

> Very little in which the teacher is expected to do calls for the awareness of the child as a constantly changing person. The steps are marked off in terms of what achievement levels are scored, not as if they reflected the child's development in a personal continuum but as a means of placing each child in a box in comparison with other children, both in the specific class and in the universal class set up for that age group. (p. 90)

Children are constantly changing persons. With the depersonalization due to crowding in the classroom and now these product-oriented images, it is easy to forget that in the center are constantly changing persons who:

should not be deprived of the control of their unique life-space, and their experience should not be compartmentalized, regimented, or trivialized in the name of efficiency, economy, and predictability. (Yamamoto, 1975, p. 117)

Ashton-Warner (1963) responded to learners as beings by teaching organically, helping children read and write "organic vocabulary," words and phrases uniquely theirs. To view learners and learning this way is challenging and less efficient than in the product view. In the same vein, Marshall (1963) writes:

To control a class in freedom, to learn with each child instead of instructing a passive class, to be a well of clear water into which the children can dip all the time, instead of a hosepipe dousing them with facts, is the most exhausting way of all of doing a teacher's job. (p. 42)

Push and pull, predict and program as we may, teaching is unpredictable in terms of both the process and the results. It is described by Jackson (1968) as an "opportunistic process" in which

the path of educational progress more closely resembles the flight of a butterfly than the flight of a bullet. (pp. 166-7)

Postman and Weingartner (1969) are among those who find the present sequential and spiral models for the learning process inadequate and prefer to compare it instead to

a Jackson Pollock canvas—a canvas whose colors increase in intensity as intellectual power grows (for learning *is* exponentially cumulative). (p. 31)

As we consider images of learners we must confront the issue of sexual stereotypes and sexual differences. While we do not want to promote the traditional sex role stereotypes, we cannot ignore actual sexual differences and treat children as if they were neuters. Sexual differences may be attributed to biological causes, parental or societal expectations, and modeling of observed sex roles. Studies continue to be made to determine real differences in a biological sense as opposed to a societal sense. Our purpose here is to determine as best we can how sexual differences affect a child's experience of school time and space.

Eleanor Maccoby and Carol Jacklin have thoroughly analyzed the general subject in their book *The Psychology of Sex Differences* (1974). McCune and Matthews (1976) summarize the actual sex differences Maccoby and Jacklin found in this way:

1. Males are more aggressive than females (boys are more aggressive physically and verbally).
2. Girls have greater verbal ability than boys.
3. Boys excell in visual-spatial ability.
4. Boys excel in mathematical ability.
   [Note: These ability differences usually do not first appear in early childhood but have their onset at adolescence and increase through the high school years.] (p. 180)

Developmental differences have been noted by other writers. Feeney (1966) notes that in the development of hand muscles boys are "a good 16 months behind girls" (p. 9). Bentzen (1966) observes that:

at the chronological age of 6, when most youngsters begin to attend school, girls are approximately 12 months ahead of boys in developmental age; by the time they are 9 years of age, this developmental differential increases to about 18 months. (p. 16)

In our efforts to be democratic and liberated, we try to treat all equally, but by doing so we may overlook some significant differences and indeed do harm rather than the intended good. How frustrating handwriting is to the child whose muscles are not ready to do it! Boys and girls are taught this subject at the same time, even though boys are a year to a year and a half behind the girls in their development.

As we make our images of learners, we will need to include sexual differences. This should occur naturally if we are responding to the individual child as a unique, growing, and changing being.

Images and Room Arrangements

Especially pertinent to our present concern are Getzels's pairings of images of the learner and room arrangement shapes (1975, pp. 1-14). He ties the empty learner image to the rectangular room arrangement. In these classroom designs, which were the standard in the early 1900s and continue to be the most prevalent today, the teacher's function is to fill the learners with knowledge. Hence all desks face front in evenly spaced rows toward the front of the class and the source of knowledge, the teacher and his or her desk.

Getzels next connects the image of the active learner to the square room arrangement. In these rooms furniture is movable, arrangements are changed, the teacher's desk joins those of the children, and the learner becomes the center. The learner in this setting is described as:

> a tumultuous bundle of needs, values, persuasions, projections, repressions, and conscious, preconscious, and unconscious psychic forces that determined his behavior. (p. 5)

Getzels's third model is the social learner and the circular classroom: "Learning was perceived as occurring through interpersonal actions and reactions. . . . " (p. 7). It is in such a shape that many of today's affective education programs occur. One commercial affective education curriculum guide even calls its program "The Magic Circle." Children learn about their own feelings, the feelings of others, and study levels and consequences of interactions.

Getzels's final model is the stimulus-seeking learner and the open classroom. This design is becoming more common as communities venture into open plan architecture where learning centers, communally owned furniture, private study places, and public areas replace classrooms, halls, and traditional school furniture. The learner is seen as "a problem finding and stimulus seeking organism" (p. 10).

Schools as Feminine Space

As we consider matching learning styles with learning environments, we cannot ignore the mismatch between many boys and their schools. Schools continue to be staffed predominantly by female teachers and male principals. Sexton (1965) writes:

> The problem is not just that teachers are too often women. It is that the school is too much a woman's world, governed by women's rules and standards. The school code is that of propriety, obedience, decorum, cleanliness, physical and, too often, mental passivity. (p. 57)

The result of this problem is that many boys dislike school, do poorly in school, and leave it as soon as possible. Another result that may be surprising is that boys develop character, independence, and autonomy from their school discomfort. They gain more of teachers' attention, both positive and negative, and they have to test themselves more than girls do. The happy consequence is that they grow significantly in personal terms, if not in schooling terms.

Girls are also affected by the feminine space. They feel natural and comfortable in the environment and do very well academically and socially. But their comfort takes its toll, for they become less willing to take risks, more dependent upon authority, and less adventurous students. Maccoby (1963) describes six-year-olds who are likely to increase their IQs by the age of ten as "competitive, self-assertive, independent, and dominant in interaction with other children. The children who show declining IQs during the next four years are children who are passive, shy, dependent" (p. 33). Frazier and Sadker (1973, p. 96) make the alarming connection for us between the behavior teachers promote and the passive, shy, dependent child whose IQ is likely to decline. That teachers are more successful with girls in this respect is especially disturbing.

So it is to everyone's benefit that school spaces be defeminized. This may easily be done by hiring more male teachers. Encouraging teachers to be more aware of the ways that they are feminizing space may also help. Grambs and Woetjen (1966) write:

> Women *literally do not know* that they use words differently, structure space differently, and perceive persons and reality differently from men. (p. 64)

Lee (1976) suggests a delightfully challenging first-aid type of solution. He acknowledges that ideally male teachers are the best models for boys and female teachers the best for girls but recognizes that we are a long way from reaching such a balance in our school faculties. He suggests:

> Essentially, then, female teachers have to develop their capacity for androgynous behavior (as should the few male teachers available to young children). . . . All it means, quite concretely, is that the female teacher get into the kind of things stereotypically associated with

males, like playing with worms and toads, having a tolerance for messes, tinkering with mechanical devices, enjoying gross motor games and sports; and she should dress accordingly. (p. 191)

To facilitate this transition it would be helpful to observe men teachers in their own classrooms and to note the different teaching methods and activities. For instance, a two-man teaching team in a sixth-grade classroom observed in Rochester, New York, works in a way strikingly different from their women colleagues. For study breaks during the day children wrestle on a rug with their teachers or throw balls at mini baskets hung strategically around the room. The classroom bulletin boards are filled with newspaper clippings, and news gathering is a significant part of the curricula.

Lee cautions us in this effort by explaining that androgynous does not mean "unisex" or that women should become exactly like men. Rather he defines it as meaning "one's sex is not the primary determinant of one's behavior, values, or aspirations" (p. 191). If both women and men respond in this way, the schools could be regarded as having human or people space rather than feminine space, and children should benefit accordingly.

School Philosophies and Styles

As a result of opposing images of the learner, differing time tense preferences, and varying educational philosophies, we have in schools today a wide array of styles and practices. Further, many schools are in a state of flux, moving toward an open structure and concept or shifting back to a more conservative position. The economic base for the differences of the past is being superseded by a philosophical one today.

An excellent source of clear descriptions of existing schools ranging along the spectrum of traditional to modern is a study made by Biber and Minuchin (1970). The philosophies and practices of four schools—three public and one private—with similar school populations and located in the same city are compared and examined for the purpose of distinguishing their impacts on child development.*

---

*The findings and implications of this interesting study are complex and significant, calling for a more thorough examination than can be given here. The reader is urged to refer to Biber and Minuchin's article (1970) or the book by Minuchin et al. (1969).

Each school's style differs in degree from the others from traditional to modern. I will consider here their descriptions of the two schools at either end of the order. First, the traditional

> Browning appeared, on the whole, untouched in its traditionalism, almost a pure form. There was minimal variety in the program—almost no activities that would be classified as creative and very little occasion to leave the classroom in which a sober, conscientious, quiet, orderly climate was consistently maintained for passively learning children. (p. 37)

And the modern

> The program was diversified; creative arts were a built-in feature of school life. . . .classrooms were busy, active places full of things in the process of being made, ideas in process of being formed, and skills being mastered, with a teacher-leader and participant children keeping as much calm as was necessary for learning and work to be unhampered—what has been described as a workshop atmosphere. (pp. 38-39)

The other two schools in the study fall between these two, and as we consider what exists today, we may decide that most schools we know would fall between them also.

Teacher Styles

Closely related to school styles are the classroom styles of teachers. Teachers' conceptions of their roles as teachers will shape their actions in the classroom. It may be helpful to see the gamut of "good" teachers as presented in educational literature. Adams and Biddle (1970) discuss two alternative images:

> One is the image of the teacher as the charismatic leader who, by force of personality, demands and gets awesome and single-minded attention while she enthralls everyone with her own virtuosity. The other is the image of the "empathetic" [sic] teacher, who somehow always seems to appreciate your thoughts, your feelings, your problems so that inevitably your learning is *personally* relevant and meaningful. (p. 86)

The last of the filters on action are teaching drawbacks. A

teacher's attitude and behavior may be influenced slightly or greatly by these. Inherent within the present role of teachers are disadvantages that need to be viewed openly. To be blunt, teaching can be very frustrating, lonely, and intellectually stymieing.

The source of the frustration is a dilemma that Sarason (1971) describes well:

> a major problem of the teacher inheres in the interaction between number and diversity of children, on the one hand, and the felt need to adhere to a time schedule, on the other hand. (p. 154)

Number and diversity of students may be problems at all levels of teaching. How can college and secondary teachers affect and guide each of their 120 students in a few hours each week? For elementary teachers the number of students is less but the assignment is a total one, all the subjects, all the time. In all teaching situations the job can never be done completely; in all, some students will not receive the time and instruction they need. Hence the frustration caused by the difference between intention and accomplishment.

Loneliness varies from teacher to teacher, from school to school. It is an unexpected drawback for a profession that is concerned with the education and welfare of others. Rewarding and lasting relationships may develop between teachers and students; however, the teacher's present obligation to instruct and evaluate and the student's present requirement to learn and perform inhibit or limit the full development of such relationships. The transitory nature of the school situation is another limitation. Relationships that grew during the year may weaken during the summer and disappear the following year as contact is reduced at each point.

The teacher's most stable source for companionship is with colleagues. However, in most schools the arrangement of time and space discourages such relationships. Unless teachers are in a teaming situation or in an open school, they are isolated from other teachers and bound to their classrooms for the better part of the day. Special class instructions may free teachers from classroom duties once a day, but because these are given in a staggered shift, few teachers are freed during the same time period. Such breaks are often spent alone in the room straightening supplies, keeping records, evaluating work, planning lessons, or preparing materials for upcoming lessons. The hours spent before and after school are used in a similar manner or spent tutoring children or supervising their activities. Teachers do manage to have social exchanges with each other at lunch, if they are not expected to eat with their classes, and in the teachers' room when they attempt to combine talk with their paper work during breaks. Discussions of much depth are difficult under such conditions and with such time limits.

In speaking with very young teachers about these matters, Sarason (1971) notes:

> They are quite unprepared both for the loneliness of the classroom and the lack of relationships in which questions and problems can be asked and discussed without the fear that the teacher is being evaluated. (p. 171)

Sarason relates the fear of evaluation back to the teacher's sense of inadequacy due to the frustration discussed above.

Closely related to this loneliness is the lack of intellectual stimulation for teachers in such settings and under such schedules. The lack of opportunity for thoughtful discussions with other faculty members represents one source. The press of clerical work and steady march of day-long school sessions to be planned occupy evening hours—this is another source. The intellectual stimulation that comes from reading literature, discussing politics, attending plays and films, or watching television must be sacrificed to evening school preparations. How insulated a teacher may become!

Finally, as Jackson (1968) has noted, when teachers are actually in their classrooms doing their jobs, the interruptions and different needs and demands of 25 individuals can mount so that teachers will engage in an astounding number of quick exchanges. It is unfortunate, though, that Jackson resigns teachers to their fate and finds a curious pleasure in seeing a fit between teachers "with all of their intellectual fuzziness and sticky sentimentality" (p. 152) and the pressing demands of classrooms. He writes:

> If teachers sought a more thorough understanding of their world, insisted on greater rationality in their actions, were completely

open-minded in their consideration of pedagogical choices, and profound in their view of the human condition, they might well receive
greater applause from intellectuals, but it is doubtful that they would
perform with greater efficiency in the classroom. On the contrary . . .
(p. 149)

Such thinking deserves the same labels that Jackson applies to
teachers, "fuzziness" and "sentimentality." He overlooks the possibility that classroom life, with its demands for shallow thinking, may
be contributing to the breakdown of teachers' intellectual acuteness.
Further, he seems unaware of teachers' possible desires to change
the situation. Instead, he regards teachers somewhat paternal-
istically as softening features in the classrooms and as models of
"human fallibility" (p. 153) for the children.

While I disagree with Jackson's interpretations, I do agree with
his observation that teachers do not always perform in intellectually
impressive ways in their classrooms. The observation calls for responses different from his; the situation as such does not always
intellectually challenge the teacher. The sameness of required curricula or grade level may also stymie intellectual liveliness.

The quality of teachers' lives, both in the classroom and out, directly affects the lives of the children in the classroom. So often
educational writers, in their conscientious efforts to view classrooms
as humanistically as possible, forget to consider the humanness of
the teacher. If a teacher is to be that "well of clear water into which
the children can dip all the time" (Marshall, 1963, p. 42), there
need to be opportunities for replenishment. By caring for ourselves,
we teachers will have more to offer our children.

THE EYE OF CHANGE: A PROCESS VIEW

Formulating the Problem

The better we question, the clearer our answers will be, say Postman and Weingartner (1969, p. 81). Our solutions are dependent
upon how we formulate the problem, adds Sarason (1971). So we
now must begin to question. What can we, as teachers, do with what
we have learned from this book? What do we want for ourselves and
our students? How can we improve the space and time in our
classrooms and schools? And as we find answers, we will need to

question again. Are they the only answers? Are they really good answers? Are they working?

What I find reassuring in this process is the fact that there is no sugar mountain in the sky that we are not seeing because of clouds of ignorance or misdirection! There are no all-time right answers. Life is real and earthbound. Students die, teachers die. What is and what is hoped for exist in a tension in a temporal world. It is within our own power to grapple with that tension, and indeed it is a sad forfeiture if we do not.

Others' Views

The solutions offered by others through their own experiences, while interesting, will not satisfy us, for *we* must be a part of the process. We cannot passively observe the works of talented teachers like Marshall, Ashton-Warner, Kohl, Holt, Cullum, or anyone else and hope to change our own classrooms into imitations of theirs. They do not ask us to do this, and we are not able to. Each of us is as different as we know each of our students to be. We can tune in to other teachers and see what they are doing and why, but then we must shift from our passive stance to an active one, determining which of their ideas relate to ourselves and our situations. We need to consider our own image of the learner, our own time preference balance, our own view of classroom life. Then the formulating, grappling, experimenting, and evaluating can begin.

We need to ask: What do *I* want? What is right for *this* group, in *this* community, at *this* time? By asking, we become aware of *our* choices, and by knowing these, we may better choose.

Practical Possibilities

How can school space and time be made better for children? We could ask them. They could create their own designs for present or future schools as a means of giving us their views. They could be included in the construction of the classroom constitution that Sarason described. They could be given sections of the classroom to decorate as "theirs." They could design the whole room as one California sixth-grade class did (see the 1975 *Learning* article described in the readings section). Their suggestions for the daily schedule could be tried. Their school boundaries could be broken down by field trips, community projects, educational walks in town as well as in nature, and frequent visits from people outside the school community. Career education providing experiences could be arranged so that children may really see what their career choices entail. Older children could leave their classes to tutor younger children. The flow of movement within the classroom and around the building could become more natural through joint efforts of students and teachers to make it so.

How can children become more sensitive to space and time? By being included in the process of making spatial and temporal decisions. There are also an increasing number of curricular games and activities that are designed to further spatial and temporal concepts (see the curricula section of Suggested Readings). Video-taping and filmmaking projects directly involve the manipulation of time and space for effect in order to communicate or entertain. The cost of equipment for such activities is no longer prohibitive.

How can school space and time be made better for teachers? How can the drawbacks of loneliness, frustration, and intellectual stymie be relieved? In many schools cooperative efforts among special teachers and classroom teachers have brought about common free times for groups of teachers who wish to work or plan together. Some schools have given their teachers release time to participate in professional development programs. In others, teachers are encouraged to use several professional days a year to observe other schools or attend workshops or conferences. Schools may also conduct switch days during which teachers switch to a grade level they do not normally teach. Such days call for a great deal of planning between teachers, and time needs to be allotted for this; however, they can result in teachers' greater appreciation of other teachers, of the process of growth in children, and of their own classes on their return. Teaming efforts among teachers for a common unit, sharing of children for different subjects, and day-long and year-long teaming arrangements can be stimulating and enjoyable. In-service programs can be upgraded in quality so that they can become invigorating and illuminating rather than being rehashes of known materials and procedures.

Other practical possibilities for classroom arrangements, teaching methods, curricula, and school architecture are offered at the end of this chapter. Look at these, read some of the highly recommended references, but then select, consider, and formulate for yourself in your own terms.

An Impractical Dream

Now to consider the school that would answer some of my own questions. . . . It would be a school in which tired teachers could take "mental health" days and not feel guilty. When a teacher felt totally drained mentally, emotionally, or physically, he or she could take a legal mental health day. I don't think that this is a bad idea for business workers and laborers, either. Certainly many professionals already do this—doctors, lawyers, politicians, actors. They recognize the need to take a break so that they may return refreshed. In any case, in this dream school, such days would be allowed, but they would not be abused. Children would benefit for, in the teacher's absence, they would be placed in the care of a refreshed, stimulating substitute—only such a variety would be hired!—and then their teacher would return renewed.

In this dream school, the day would end at noon. Teachers would use afternoons to do the work that they now do in the evenings, and their evenings would become freed for other pursuits. The afternoons could also be used to work with other teachers or to study as students themselves.

What would the children do? Let us ask, "What would they like to do?" They would probably get bored doing nothing; they are indeed Getzels's stimulus-seeking, problem-finding organisms. A few could make those hours valuable; Tim certainly could, the student writer who dreamed that all schools are closed. Most would want to do something with other children. The few whom I have asked have said that they would spend that time playing sports. Others would prefer to do something in the arts—painting, building, acting. Working with cars, bikes, and motors, caring for animals, riding horseback, and hiking would be still other choices.

Such an afternoon program could be conducted in the school, in a community center, or perhaps in the community as a whole. The teachers could be older students, retired people, the unemployed, or professional people released from their work for short periods of time. Parents could participate as teachers for their own and others' children. Children could become teachers. Teachers might wish to participate as students of their students. Artists, cooks, pilots, carpenters, writers, road builders, dress designers, test drivers, mechanics, lumbermen, conservationists, singers, dancers, and scientists could show children what they do at work. The old and the young would mix as they do in the world. An array of career choices and life styles would be displayed to the children. And the children would be able to participate in these activities and many others— mechanical, athletic, artistic, social service, academic, or what have you.

The dream may be impractical for the moment, but by considering it, we may find some ways, some other choices.

The Eye of Change

The teacher is at the center of any school change that organically affects his or her classroom. The teacher can better see the needs of children and has a better sense of classroom life. There are questions to be asked and changes to seek. The tension between what is and what could be needs to be grappled with. And teachers need to be active centers in the process.

Suggested Practices and Readings

Room Arrangements

Flexible grouping

For example, a circle for group discussions, two facing rows for debates, small desk groupings for team projects, individual islands for independent study, close huddles for brainstorming, as well as free selection for films and group presentations. Several of these may be used in the course of one day by letting the activity determine the seating arrangement.

A totally student-designed classroom

An example is the sixth-grade classroom, taught by Mel Prowse and described by Westerberg (1975). It is complete with student-made lofts, stage coach and western jail study spots, and poster collaged walls. Time and space are organized in unconventional, intriguing ways. The article is worth reading.

Indoor innovations by designers

A good example is Curtis and Smith (1975). They found inspirations for their works in a Mexican marketplace and in their observations of the movements of children. When children requested places to crawl away into, they obliged only to discover that children still wanted to see what was going on outside their own nooks. The resulting towers and tubes, complete with plastic windows and domes, make a peaceful, open, yet private environment.

The classroom as stage for dramas

Cullum (1967) presents many possible transformations of the classroom, including one for a Joint Session of the Congress for his "parade of Presidents" social studies lessons, another as the Renoir Room in a museum, and still another as the workshop for the construction of the Trojan Horse.

Innovations in a conservative climate

West (1967), a British how-to book, is a good counterpoint to the American, feet-first attitudes toward innovation. It may indeed be a necessity for those squirming in a strictly structured school environment.

Free and zaney innovations

Farallones Designs (1971) provides a wild collection of practical tips for building imaginative classroom furnishings and also offers ideas and methods for teaching the concepts of space to children.

Curricula

Creative writing

One may ask children to project themselves into the future and describe schools, cities, or future life in general. Good sources of inspiration for such activities are Ellison (1969) and "Five Noted Thinkers Explore the Future" (1976).

Mathematics

History and the workings of the time-measuring devices may be explored. In pairs, children may try to infer the duration to the second of one minute, three minutes, and so on.

Critical thinking

Have children project today's problems into the future, and consider methods of solving them. Note the ways in which our society structures time and space, and weigh alternatives. Some of these alternatives may be found in other cultures.

Room and schedule planning

Ask children's ideas for room arrangements and activity scheduling. Integrate these into planning whenever possible and desirable. See, for instance, Renfro (1976).

Classroom extension

Videotaping and filmmaking projects help break down the boundaries between school and home or school and the world. One good source is Whitcomb (1974).

Career education

Opportunities for the creation of future-focussed role images (Singer, 1974). The practice of "shadowing"—following someone through a work day—is a useful form of career education.

Literature

The time orientations of different writers may be examined in terms of their effectiveness and pertinence to the explicit or implicit themes.

Environmental education

For an excellent collection of programs, see "Environmental Education from Kindergarten On Up" (1969).

School Environments

Green, Alan C. "Planning for Declining Enrollments." In Thomas G. David and Benjamin D. Wright (Eds.), *Learning environments.* Chicago: University of Chicago Press, 1975. Pp. 69–74.

Not far from my Fellini dream. The author states: "There is a growing tendency when planning school facilities to make common cause with other social services—the arts, recreation, day care, libraries, job training, health, and on and on. The emerging cooperative art form is the community/school or the community center . . ." (p. 71)

The *Harvard Educational Review,* 1969, *39,* 1–147.

This whole Fall 1969 issue (number 4) is devoted to the topic, "Architecture and Education." Of the articles, the following are of special interest:

Carew, Topper. "Interview," pp. 98–147.

These interviews were conducted by Arthur Blackman, Ken Freidus, David Robinson, and Florence Shelton Ladd. One of the first store-front schools, "The New Thing," is described and the underlying philosophy discussed.

Goodman, Robert. "Liberated Zone: An Evolving Learning Space," pp. 86–97.

An architect, his students, and high school youngsters plan together a learning space for the high school students.

Hertzberger, Herman. "Montessori Primary School in Delft, Holland," pp. 58–67.

This well illustrated article shows a school that "has been made to answer the specific demands of a non-traditional teaching system." (p. 58)

Holt, John. *What do I do Monday?* New York: Dell, 1970.

A mobile learning environment is described in "New Spaces for Learning," pp. 282–292.

Toffler, Alvin (Ed.) *Learning for tomorrow: The role of the future in education.* New York: Vintage, 1974.

A mixture of articles tied together by a common valuing of futurism.

*The journey through the kaleidoscopic matrices of
time and space is an experience common to all human
beings. The last chapter by a noted curriculum
theorist looks at this shared endeavor as a way of
summarizing the whole book. She asks how the young
and old may learn from each other to enrich the
precious gift of life throughout their existence on this
earth. After all, this is what education is about, is it not?*

Child of the Moment, Child of Eternity:

From Generation to Generation

LOUISE M. BERMAN

A child enters life in a moment, lives a series of moments, and later departs in a moment. Eternity lies before and behind the child. During the sojourn on earth, the existential dilemma is how to live days fully, compassionately, expansively, and responsively while simultaneously giving attention to questions of eternity. Questions asked are usually specific to the child's time and space: Where did I come from? Where am I going? With whom will I travel? What shall I do as I pass through time and space?

Even as the child ponders such questions, so does the person in middle age or later life. In addition to the previous questions, the older person might query: Does what I do matter? What else should I do in the moments left to me? What if I could recapture the many moments that have slipped away? How would I use them differently?

Since persons of all ages possess certain perspectives on matters relating to time and space, it stands to reason that experiences shared by persons in different stages of life should add richness for all. Persons from different generations, therefore, need time to work together, reflect together, laugh together, cry together, plan together, care together—indeed, just to *be* together!

In societies unencumbered by highly industrialized and technological advances, planned attention to intergenerational living, thinking, and communicating may not be as necessary. To carry out daily tasks, persons of all ages may be found in common meeting places. Young boys work with their fathers in the fields; young girls carry out household chores with their mothers. All persons come together for some events. Interaction among generations comes about through daily living.

When societies move to more complex structures, specialization becomes important, and peer grouping by age replaces many of the heterogeneous groupings of more simple societies. The lack of fertilization of ideas across age lines may result in all persons acquiring dwarfed concepts about the meaning of time.

The purpose of this chapter then is threefold: (1) to uncover some of the richness of ideas about time as considered by philosophers, natural scientists, and students of human behavior; (2) to consider persons in various stages of the life cycle and how their sense of time can enhance the child's understanding of temporality; and (3) to offer practical suggestions for those who are now exploring what it means to be a child of the moment and of eternity.

CONCEPTIONS OF TIME

Throughout the ages, perceptions and utilization of time have strongly influenced the development of people within societies. Whatever the value placed upon time, it is "the dimension of the universe that allows things to happen" (MacIver, 1962, p. 2).

In post-figurative societies, or those societies in which children learn primarily from their forebearers (Mead, 1970), we find a lack of questioning and a lack of consciousness. Time does not evoke shifts in meaning. A "network of mutual obligations" exists (Doob, 1971, p. 53); the future is anticipated with accuracy, but anticipation ordinarily is passive involving little intervention. For example, peasants may plan for their children in terms of how their fathers and grandfathers planned for them.

Persons living in industrialized societies usually are very much aware of clock time or outer time. Temporal awareness involves thinking about making active use of the moments. Passive acceptance of time gives way to active involvement in time. Whether time is seen as something that engulfs people and over which they have little control or whether time is seen as dimensions of life over which individuals have at least partial control, a glimpse of certain aspects of time may be useful. Views of time as moment, as duration, as change, and as imagined future will be briefly considered.

Time as Moment

According to Webster, a moment is a tiny or minute portion of time. Moments are atomistic and frequently are referred to as instants or as *now*. From the Latin word *momentum*, the derivation of the word is the same as for the words motion and influence. Thus moments cause us to become aware of the passage or movement of time and the influence of one moment upon another. Moments ordinarily have linkages. These linkages are variously referred to as rhythms, occurrences, intervals, events, time series, or duration — chunks of time (Cottle and Klineberg, 1974; Lucas, 1973). Thus, if moments merge into duration, how the present moment should be lived becomes a critical question for persons of all generations.

It is important that the young have moments full of vivid experiences — of seeing a beautiful sunset, of feeling a splash of cold water, of feeling the texture of moist clay. Young persons need moments that promote personal growth, else they will say like the prostitute, "You can't have a full life when the beginning gets all messed up" (Cottle and Klineberg, 1974, p. 124). Adults need moments of introspection and stocktaking so that they can use the moments left to them to create new goals and purposes and move toward their fulfillment.

It is from instants that material for one's personal storage box of memories is created. If the instants are poorly filled, the box may contain isolated and fragmented events. Well-filled, the box may hold incidents that make duration worthwhile.

Time as Duration

The succession of ideas, memories, instants, or events is important in time, for duration arises through reflecting on a train of ideas (Ornstein, 1969; Sherover, 1975). An instant is an instantaneous event whose beginning and end are not perceived in our experience of it. The succession of ideas or duration is a fundamental experience. From succession emerges all time concepts. In essence, time is the way we measure and compare "chunks" of duration. In other words, duration refers to lastingness.

Most human societies have some way of describing duration. For example, a week may be anywhere from three to 16 or more days. Weeks grow into months and months into years. For duration to be significant, it must have meaning for the persons living through it. In some areas of the world, the division of time is based upon the social life of a people, such as market days. Lived time matters more than astronomical time.

Many factors influence the significance of duration. For example, duration is usually more significant when persons see others as individuals to be loved rather than objects to serve some preconceived end (Buber, 1958, 1965). Duration is more meaningful when persons are seeking the same or similar goals and must cooperate or coordinate activities to achieve them (Doob, 1971). Engaging in common projects within a community, helping a family member with a problem, or reaching across state or national boundaries to participate in a project are ways in which people can learn to care across age boundaries. The duration of time can then be meaningful for all.

Duration is also likely to have import when the power relations between groups or individuals are considered. Children demonstrate power with adults when they attempt to control them by screaming, fighting, or refusing to carry out a task. On the other hand, children are also powerful when they persuade adults to accommodate to them through sweetness and kindness. Likewise adults demonstrate their power through the schedules they try to establish, the rules or boundaries they try to set, or the acts of selflessness they perform. Time as worthwhile duration is seen when attention is given to the wise sharing of power among all persons within a setting. Mead (1970) advocates a considered and careful sharing of power among young and old so that we move ahead in shaping societies fit for all.

Instants or moments may fade from view, but duration has permanence. Duration may be short-term or long-term; it provides for continuity, for links among the instants and intervals so that the pieces make sense.

Time as Change

Change refers to the process of altering, modifying, converting, or varying. The passing of time is a constant, but the rate at which things, persons, or situations are altered or modified in time is variable. Human beings are the only creatures who can make change continuous or discontinuous, for individuals have the ability to intervene in their environment. Change, unlike moments and duration, deals with discontinuities that may be abrupt or gradual, anticipated or unanticipated.

At times change may be almost imperceptible. Consider a river. The banks remain almost constant, changing ever so slowly. Yet a river may flow very swiftly, change taking place at a rapid pace.

At other times change may be very dramatic. According to Doob (1971), in religious conversion a central trait is changed. A person may be transformed and thus perceive her or his milieu in a different way.

Change may also be noted when a person for one reason or another loses someone close. It can be noted in the behavior of individuals when a reallocation of resources means that some persons within an organization are going to be laid off. Shifts in behavior or changes also occur when people, either as a result of their own choosing or someone choosing for them, are relocated.

Human groups go on in time, but groups shift and change. As individuals come to see and understand change in themselves and others, they can better appreciate the perspectives that persons of different generations have on life and living.

Time as Imagined Future

Who am I? Where am I going? What do I hope to accomplish in life? What are the settings in which I might find myself? What are some alternative futures? These and related questions cause individuals to reflect on what lies ahead and to contemplate future time.

Persons can plan alternative futures and contemplate necessary steps to achieving them. Organizations such as the World Future Society and writers such as Teilhard de Chardin (1964), Toffler (1974), Bell (1973), and Michael (1973) offer provocative ways of thinking about the future. For example, people can consider alternative kinds of communities, careers, values, and families. What life styles will be appropriate ten years hence? What are some new values that need to be created if we are to survive on planet earth? What are some satisfying ways in which people can group themselves in communities? What are some new careers currently being developed? If a person were to enter a specified career, what changes over time would need to take place in his or her life?

Hope, faith, and rational planning are necessary qualities in thinking about future time. Dreams can become visions implemented through ventures. These ventures can later be lived as exciting moments and seen in retrospect as worthwhile events or duration. Individuals from different generations together can imagine futures and thus create fresh, possible worlds.

CROSSING GENERATIONS: ADVENTURES IN TIME

Generation is derived from the same root word as generating or creating. Individuals interacting from different generations can draw upon the stored wisdom of the mature, capitalize on the freshness of spirit of the young, and create anew on the basis of the strengths of all. Generations in collaboration have opportunities to live life so that time is well spent. Individuals can acquire such understandings as: (1) it is impossible to think of something in time without something preceding it; (2) the links in time are as naturally ordered as the successive states of infancy, adolescence, and maturity; and (3) no element in the universe is wholly independent of its nearby threads (Teilhard de Chardin, 1964).

All human beings are given moments, live through time as duration, are aware of change, and can imagine the future. People from all generations are constantly moving ahead in time—but never back. All live with the realization that time is a necessary commodity if goals and purposes are to be realized. Yet in different stages of development, they may have different perspectives on time. What might characterize the perspectives of individuals in early, middle, and later life?

Early Life

A four-year-old, traveling with her grandparents, stopped for lunch in a restaurant:

> "I want some cake," said the child.
> "You will have it when you get to grandmother's," said the grandmother.
> "But I want it now! Right now!"

All of us who have contact with young children are familiar with the "nowness" of this generation. As mentioned in earlier chapters, a young child typically chooses something at hand over a distant prize, which may be greater than the immediately available one.

As children grow into adolescence, they begin to struggle with problems of nowness as opposed to delayed gratification. Some youth may prefer to delay financial ventures until they have had the opportunity to pursue higher education. According to Cottle and Klineberg (1974), "As each of us becomes acutely aware of the irreversibility and finitude of our lives, we are faced with the same broad questions: Shall we choose the immediate reward, or work instead for the remoter but greater one?" (p. 194).

Much of what we know about how children perceive time comes from their reporting of it. Because their verbal skills are not yet fully developed, one can only infer much about their orientation to time. Lack of verbal expertise on the part of the young confounds what we know about their understanding of time. Furthermore we do not know *why* young children report or do not report about matters pertaining to time.

Up until two years of age, one can glean faint hints that children perceive a past or future time but at two, the child may say words indicating an awareness of a future, e.g., "In a minute," or "I'm going to . . .," or "Wait!"

At three years of age the child may talk in the past, present, and future. Children can now tell how old they are, when they go to bed, what they will do at Christmas, and the like.

At five, the child can ordinarily handle the days of the week and at six knows the four seasons. At seven years the child can handle specific clock hours. At eight the young can begin to ponder, "What does time mean?" (Ames, 1946; Orme, 1968). One cannot but wonder whether digital clocks and watches make the perception of clock time any easier.

At 12 or 13, appreciation of duration becomes more accurate. Early adolescents begin to show the fruits of their thinking about time in their planning for the future. They can plan accurately only in terms of events that possess meaning for them. It should be noted also that as children become older, there is less wish fulfilling fantasy, less interest in material acquistions, and more emphasis on educational or vocational goals (Lessing, 1968).

Middle Life

Although experts in human development have given much attention to the young, little attention has been paid to the developmental process of those in middle life. This is a significant group, for they ordinarily have responsibility for both the young and the elderly. Sheehy (1974) has pointed out that this stage of life has just as many developmental crises as any other period, yet we have failed to be concerned about these crises. Other members of society have given the person in middle life a cloak of steadiness, sense of responsibility, and maturity. The "ups and downs" of this age group are thought to be minor.

If we remove the stereotypes attributed to middle life, quite different images of these people may emerge. The child who has opportunity to interact on fundamental issues with persons in middle life may gain many insights about time and its meaning for life.

For example, as one moves into middle life, he or she moves from simple role demands to highly complex ones. Yet seldom are the skills needed to assume more complex and conflicting roles taught. That the passage of time brings more moments of complexity is an important learning for the young.

Related to the increasing complexity of roles is learning that persons in middle life receive increasingly unclear rewards (Brim and Wheeler, 1966). The child frequently is given immediate approval or disapproval for what he or she does. Yet those in middle life, functioning in complex roles, may receive insignificant or unclear signals relative to the quality and worth of their actions. How frustrating such conditions may be, yet how much better can children meet the adult world if they are aware that persons "in charge" carry out conflicting and challenging tasks with few clear external rewards.

Even as young people are busy setting goals, so persons in middle life frequently reappraise their goals. Were the goals too low? Too lofty? If they were achieved, were they worth achieving? Now that time is running out, what new goals ought to be set? What parts of one's life have been sacrificed to achieve certain goals? Does one want to continue to suppress the same parts of life? How can one generate new worthwhile goals in life? These and other questions plague men and women in middle life who come to see sharply and clearly that time is finite and life does not provide enough days to accomplish all the goals set in earlier years.

The person who reaches early middle life and finds life gratifying might find it difficult to move toward another stage of development (Bocknek, 1976). Birthdays, anniversaries, and holidays put persons in touch with the passage of time. That one must leave a satisfying stage of life to move onto another stage may prove frustrating. For example, students may prefer to stay within the sheltered walls of academe rather than to try to apply what they have learned. The employed person may prefer sticking with a job he or she knows to trying a new, potentially more promising one. The lover may prefer casual relationships to the more enduring marriage relationship. The child can learn from the middle-aged person that it is normal to be reluctant to leave a gratifying stage of life; yet new satisfactions can come with each new era.

Because of the complexity of roles, the lack of a clear reward system, and the necessity of making one's own decisions about when to move to next steps, the individual in middle life frequently looks

inward rather than outward to find answers to questions or solutions to problems. The increased saliency of the inner life has been
referred to as "interiority" (Neugarten, 1976, p. 17). As duration of
time allows memories to be sorted and stored, individuals can draw
upon past impressions, periods of change, and enduring personal
values in moving from one phase of life to another. The child can
begin to see that one is not grown up at 18 or 19, but rather that
each new period in life calls for a reappraisal of where one has been
and where one is going.

Finally, the finiteness of time is sensed in middle life. Death becomes a real possibility, and its effect not only in the self but also on
others is contemplated. That life no longer stretches endlessly ahead
becomes poignantly clear.

Thus, middle life is a time of stock taking, goal reviewing, and
contemplating one's finiteness. For the young to be able to talk with,
know, care for, and ponder persons who are experiencing life mid-
stream is indeed a worthwhile experience. For those in middle life to
be able to listen to the dreams of the young, their confessions, and
their hopes means that joint planning for the future can take place.

Later Life

People in later life may possess an awareness that in reality a
lengthy future does not lie before them. "Some avoid confronting
this fact by retreating to the past. . . . Others deny their age and
continue to be future-oriented. The latter are people who fail to
make wills, who leave important relationships unresolved, who put
off enjoyments, who experience the boredom and frustration that
can come from never fully experiencing the present" (Butler, 1975,
p. 409). Persons in later life may resolve the shortness of the re-
mainder of their lives through viewing time as quality rather than
as quantity, an important learning for the young.

As older persons seek out qualitative kinds of experiences, they
sense the life cycle, and death may become a center leading to
creativity or despair. Time becomes more subjective than objective
as individuals sort through their memory banks and review what
has taken place in their lifetimes. Sorting out ideas and memories
may lead to a desire to preserve continuity, leave a legacy, and
transmit power.

For many, old age presents opportunities for new experiences and for creativity. Fresh learnings as well as the integration of past meanings can be part of the person in later life. As children interact with older people, they can begin to see that success can be measured in the overall quality of life rather than only in the acquisition of things. Children can see the possibilities that time presents for reconciliation of person with person, for integrating old and new ideas, and for experiencing continuities and discontinuities in human existence.

CHILD OF THE MOMENT, CHILD OF ETERNITY

An assumption has been made that, through planning for cross-generational interaction, children (and adults) can gain a better perspective on time and its meaning for human living. A corollary assumption is that interaction among persons from different generations should promote better cross-generational communication and caring. What follows are a few suggestions for helping children gain a richer conception of time as they deal with the human condition. It should be noted that in providing opportunities for children to develop a sense of time, emphasis is on processes such as contributing, planning, and reaching out. The total experience rather than only the end product is important (Berman, 1968; Berman and Roderick, 1977; Frazier, 1976a, 1976b).

Give children opportunities to reach out *to persons older and younger than themselves.* In the short story, "100 Handkerchiefs" by Christine Miskovits (1972), the reader can identify with 16-year-old Marsha who reaches out to her grandmother's friend, Miss Holloway, following her grandmother's death. Other delightful stories can be found in which children have a deep relationship with an older person. See, for example, Judy Blume's *Are You There God? It's Me, Margaret* (1970), or Fynn's *Mister God, This Is Anna* (1974).

Many schools make it possible for the old and the young to develop reciprocal relationships through Grandparents Programs. In such programs a child is assigned to a senior citizen who comes to school on a voluntary but regular basis to engage in various activities with the child. Both the young and the old stand to benefit by the interchange. Both directly and indirectly, the child can begin to get a feeling for time as duration and change, especially if the tasks in which young and old work side by side invite the older person to share something of her or his experiences.

Give individuals opportunities to see how nature, literature, music, drama, and media depict aspects of the life cycle and the phenomenon of change. A consideration of different ages, different life styles, and different cultures as conceived by writers, artists, or musicians can give insight into the nature of change. Stories that show persons at different stages in the life cycle and art forms that capture youth, middle life, or old age can be useful in trying to get a grasp of the change process. Stories that focus upon crisis, and upon what transpires following a crisis experience, can sharpen awareness as to what stimulates change. People who live in parts of the world where a change of seasons exists can come to understand change through observing seasonal changes in nature.

Provide opportunities for persons of all ages to look *carefully at others and to* analyze *what they see.* Through a careful look at individuals in various stages of the life cycle, persons can learn to describe qualities of individuals rather than only making generalizations about groups. For example, children might observe over a period of time three or four older persons, describe them, and then discuss how they are like and unlike others of approximately the same age.

Then children might try to look for evidences of honesty, friendliness, sharing, and caring in persons representing different ages. In this way, children can begin to see continuity in human nature.

With the current emphasis on aging, young people might be asked to search for studies such as the one conducted by Thomas and Yamamoto (1975) on attitudes toward and perceptions of the aging. Since much is currently being done to change the stereotypes of the elderly, young people might be asked to analyze studies to see the kinds of contributions they are making to our understanding of persons who have lived extended periods in time.

Ask children to elaborate *on meanings of time as moment, duration, change, and imagined futures.* Children can find examples from their daily lives, from newspapers, or from the works of poets, storytellers, and musicians that expand their concepts of time. Children can search out how industrialization and technology change the ways young, middle aged, and older persons use time. Finally, youth can be asked to consider how such concepts as hope or rational planning influence thinking about imagined futures.

Provide experiences that evoke questions *about time, continuity, and the relationship of persons to time.* Mead (1970) has indicated that one finds traditional, postfigurative societies when persons do not question. Since the pacing of modern life demands people who are constantly questioning to find better answers, conditions for children should be such that inquisitive minds are developed. Spaces rich with materials about different stages of life or utilizing persons in the classroom who come from different age groups can encourage thoughtful examination of time and its meaning for life. Children can be taught to examine learning based on answers to which there are no good questions.

Provide opportunities for individuals to reflect on their contributions *to life.* By defining commitments and working through what they wish to be their legacy, people of all ages can think intelligently about their sojourn in time. They can come to grips with their own mortality if they have had occasion to ponder their own contributions to life both in terms of people for whom they care and in terms of ideas they wish to sanction.

Help persons develop planning *abilities as a critical aspect of intelligence.* According to Orme (1968), "Intelligence is a general, cognitive function including those of memory, perception, and learning" (p. 161). All these are related to intelligence and to the past space-time organization. If we wish to be more comprehensive in our consideration of intelligence and/or basic life functions, we will give increased attention to planning. Ordinarily planning is neither taught nor evaluated, a major limitation in instruction and testing.

If we are interested in helping our young learn to plan, then we can give them experiences with persons of different ages in different stages of planning and implementing various kinds of projects. Children who learn to give attention to planning do not feel that time is passing them by. Rather feelings that one can help determine what will happen in the space of time can be evoked. Also attention to planning can help persons learn to load the moment with appropriate activity, thus avoiding living hastily or sluggishly.

Planning involves the improvement of temporal judgment, which sharpens as psychological, linguistic, and social abilities improve (Doob, 1971). The improvement of symbolic processes enables the young to communicate more easily with persons from various generations and thus to obtain from them some practical help in planning.

The young can learn from cross-generational interaction that some individuals work steadily. Others alternate between furious expenditures of energy and periods of idling. Children can learn how they work best and the rewards that come from both types of activity. They can learn that society does not plan well for the person who deviates from the norm in pacing his or her work. In helping children learn to plan, we need to keep in mind that completed tasks seem shorter than incompleted tasks; thus, one way we can assist them in learning techniques of planning is to insure that the planning provides for some degree of completion.

Give children opportunities to hear *folklore, traditions, and fantasies to develop a sense of time.* Hearing is the basic sense modality used in the perceiving of change and time. Although hearing locates things in space only vaguely, hearing locates time precisely (Orme, 1968). If hearing is so important to acquiring a time awareness, then the young need many opportunities to hear from people of various ages their excursions into time. Hearing persons tell what they would do if they could relive a segment of life or hearing family folklore can help children form a sense of continuity with others while simultaneously developing their own time sense. Families might start books of family incidents to be shared with younger generations. Tape recordings of important events in the life of a family or feelings of children at certain ages can help them develop a sense of the continuity of time.

Help young people nurture a sense of caring *so that they can develop a more realistic perspective on temporal matters.* The child who is deprived of love in his infancy may develop a poor sense of time (Orme, 1968). Such a child may later have difficulty giving and receiving affection. Children who have the advantage of constantly comparing their ideas of duration with those of a variety of ages can quickly form better and more accurate perceptions on time than those who only have the perspective of their peer group against which to match their own perceptions and their own sense of caring.

Through intergenerational contacts based upon love, children can become aware of problems caused by boredom and impatience. The bored person wants the interval to end so as to be able to turn to another activity. The impatient person wants to attain some positive or significant goal. The loving adult can recognize signs of boredom and impatience and can help redirect the child into challenges that breed fulfillment.

Provide stimulating *experiences so that children are aware of the passing of time.* When stimuli are insignificant or unclear, individuals find an inability to make sense of the time that is theirs. A need exists to find out what are intensely stimulating experiences for given individuals. Such information enables planning so that people representing different generations can provide the child with stimuli that shape moments of meaning. We frequently plan for a child's learning in terms of what we think he or she should know. Seldom do we give enough attention to what is intensely stimulating for the child. A hobby shared, a story told, an instrument played, a presence felt—these are all contributions that can be made by persons of any age to the growth of the young.

Experiences should be planned that cause children to reflect *on the meaning of eternity.* It is easier to plan for the moment of now than to plan experiences that cause children to think beyond time. Eternity is not made up of successive moments, and it is indeed difficult to wrest ourselves from thinking in terms of the moment. However, in terms of pondering the ageless, adults and children together can write biographies and autobiographies. These personal histories may at times be written alone. When the child has had an experience in common with an adult, they can write together, thus getting a feeling for the continuity of generations.

By serving as an apprentice to an adult who has a trade, by being in situations where birth, death, and life are discussed, by visiting wildernesses full of ancient trees, by investing one's self in the persistent dilemmas of life, the child begins to reflect and even dimly sense the meaning of eternity.

Rhythm, rest, recreation, renewal—these are all ways that individuals get a grasp of time. Through mental stimulation, they prepare themselves to investigate those critical areas of life that make for a full and rewarding life.

Child of the Moment, Child of Eternity. Through the collaborative pursuits of old and young, each may find fuller moments and a richer eternity.

Suggested Readings

On Time

Cottle, Thomas J., & Klineberg, Stephen L. *The present of things future: Explorations of time in human experience*. New York: Free Press, 1974.

A highly readable volume on time with chapters on developmental and socio-cultural perspectives and telling case histories.

Doob, Leonard W. *Patterning of time*. New Haven: Yale University Press, 1971.

A comprehensive treatment of time organized around the themes of "Processes," "Functioning," and "Manipulation."

Sherover, Charles M. *The human experience of time: The development of its philosophic meaning*. New York: New York University Press, 1975.

A collection of readings on such topics as "Time and Motion," "Time and Understanding," "The Analysis of Temporal Concepts," and "The Significance of Experiential Time."

On Generations in Time

Brim, Orville, B., Jr., & Wheeler, Stanton. *Socialization after childhood: Two essays*. New York: Wiley, 1966.

Brim's essay, "Socialization through the Life Cycle," is useful in understanding adult socialization—weaknesses and strengths in adult reward and role systems.

Buber, Martin. *I and thou* (2nd ed.). New York: Scribners, 1958.

A classic work that considers the relationship of one person to another that cuts across time and space.

Butler, Robert N. *Why survive? Being old in America*. New York: Harper & Row, 1975.

An informative book based upon a careful analysis of societal trends. Discusses what is, and what might be, in terms of persons in later life.

Counseling adults. *Counseling Psychologist*, 1976, *6* (1), 2–70.

Guest edited by Nancy Schlossberg, the theme of the whole issue is counseling adults. It contains worthwhile articles by such writers as Orville Brim, Bernice Neugarten, and Gene Bockneck.

Lidz, Theodore. *The person: His development through the life cycle*. New York: Basic Books, 1968.

A comprehensive treatment of the person. Deals with "The Setting," "The Life Cycle," and "Patterns and Perspectives."

Mead, Margaret. *Culture and commitment: A study of the generation gap.* Garden City: Natural History Press/Doubleday, 1970.

A useful discussion of the effect of cultures and cultural change. Culture is discussed in terms of the past, present, and future.

References

Adams, Raymond S., & Biddle, Bruce J. *Realities of teaching*. New York: Holt, 1970.

Ainsworth, Mary D. Salter, & Bell, Silvia M. Mother-infant interaction and the development of competence. In Kevin Connolly & Jerome Bruner (Eds.), *The growth of competence*. New York: Academic Press, 1974. Pp. 97–118.

Alexenberg, Melvin L. Toward an integral structure through science and art. *Main Currents in Modern Thought*, 1974, *30*, 146–152.

Allen, Vernon L. (Ed.). *Children as teachers*. New York: Academic Press, 1976.

Allport, Gordon W. *Becoming*. New Haven: Yale University Press, 1955.

Almy, Millie & Genishi, Celia. *Ways of studying children* (2nd ed.). New York: Teachers College Press, 1979.

Alvin, Juliette. *Music therapy*. New York: Basic Books, 1975.

Ames, Louise B. The development of the sense of time in the young child. *Journal of Genetic Psychology*, 1946, *68*, 97.

Armstrong, Virginia Irving. *I have spoken*. Chicago: Swallow Press, 1971.

Ashton-Warner, Sylvia. *Teacher*. New York: Simon & Schuster, 1963.

Barker, Roger G., & Gump, Paul V. *Big school, small school*. Stanford: Stanford University Press, 1964.

Baruch, Dorothy W. *One little boy*. New York: Dell, 1964.

Bauer, David H. An exploratory study of developmental changes in children's fears. *Journal of Child Psychology and Psychiatry*, 1976, *17*, 69–74.

Baumrind, Diana. The development of instrumental competence through socialization. In Ann D. Pick (Ed.), *Minnesota symposium on child psy-*

chology, Vol. 7. Minneapolis: University of Minnesota Press, 1973. Pp. 3–46.

Becker, Wesley C. Consequences of different kinds of parental discipline. In Martin L. Hoffman & Lois W. Hoffman (Eds.), *Review of child development research*, Vol. 1. New York: Russell Sage Foundation, 1964. Pp. 169–208.

Bell, Daniel. *The coming of post-industrial society: A venture into social forecasting.* New York: Basic Books, 1973.

Bentzen, Frances. Sex ratios in learning and behavior disorders. *National Elementary Principal,* 1966, *46* (2), 13–17.

Berg, Leila. *Look at kids.* Baltimore: Penguin, 1972.

Bergson, Henri. *An introduction to metaphysics: The creative mind.* Totowa, N.J.: Littlefield, Adams. 1965.

Berman, Louise M. *New priorities in the curriculum.* Columbus: Charles E. Merrill, 1968.

Berman, Louise M., & Roderick, Jessie A. *Curriculum: Teaching the what, how, and why of living.* Columbus: Charles E. Merrill, 1977.

Bertalanffy, Ludwig von. On the definition of symbol. In Joseph R. Royce (Ed.), *Psychology and the symbol.* New York: Random House, 1965. Pp. 26–72.

Bettelheim, Bruno. *The empty fortress.* New York: Free Press, 1967.

Bettelheim, Bruno. *The informed heart.* New York: Avon, 1971.

Bettelheim, Bruno. *A home for the heart.* New York: Bantam, 1975.

Bettelheim, Bruno. *The uses of enchantment.* New York: Alfred A. Knopf, 1976.

Biber, Barbara, & Minuchin, Patricia. The impact of school philosophy and practice on child development. In Norman V. Overly (Ed.), *The unstudied curriculum: Its impact on children.* Washington, D.C.: Association for Supervision and Curriculum Development, 1970. Pp. 27–52.

Blume, Judy. *Are you there, God? It's me, Margaret.* Scarsdale, N.Y.: Bradbury Press, 1970.

Bocknek, Gene. A developmental approach to counseling adults. *Counseling Psychologist,* 1976, *6*, 37–40.

Bowlby, John. *Child care and the growth of love* (2nd ed.). Baltimore: Penguin, 1965.

Bowlby, John. *Attachment and loss,* Vol. 1, *Attachment.* New York: Basic Books, 1969.

Bowlby, John. *Attachment and loss,* Vol. 2, *Separation.* New York: Basic Books, 1973.

Bradley, N. C. The growth of the knowledge of time in children of school-age. *British Journal of Psychology,* 1947, *38*, 67–78.

Bridgman, P. W. Science and common sense. *Scientific Monthly.* 1954, *82*, 32–39.

Brim, Orville. Theories of the male mid-life crisis. *Counseling Psychologist,* 1976, *6,* 2–9.

Brim, Orville G., Jr., & Wheeler, Stanton. *Socialization after childhood: Two essays.* New York: Wiley, 1966.

Bronfenbrenner, Urie. *Two worlds of childhood: U.S. and U.S.S.R.* New York: Russell Sage Foundation, 1970.

Brown, Roger. Development of the first language in the human species. *American Psychologist,* 1973, *28,* 97–106.

Bruner, Jerome. *Outline for "Man: A Course of Study."* Cambridge, Mass.: Education Development Center, 1968.

Buber, Martin. *I and thou* (2nd ed.). New York: Scribners, 1958.

Buber, Martin. *Between man and man.* New York: Macmillan, 1965.

Bühler, Charlotte. Early environmental influences on goal setting. In Charlotte Bühler & Fred Massarik (Eds.), *The course of human life; A study of goals in the humanistic perspective.* New York: Springer, 1968. Pp. 173–188.

Butler, Robert N. *Why survive? Being old in America.* New York: Harper & Row, 1975.

Caldwell, Bettye M. The effects of infant care. In Martin L. Hoffman & Lois W. Hoffman (Eds.), *Review of child development research,* Vol. 1. New York: Russell Sage Foundation, 1964. Pp. 9–87.

Calitri, Charles J. Space, time, and people in schools. *Teachers College Record,* 1975, *77,* 83–98.

Carew, Topper. Interview. *Harvard Educational Review,* 1969, *39,* 98–115.

Cassirer, Ernst. *An essay on man.* New Haven: Yale University Press, 1944.

Cassirer, Ernst. *The philosophy of symbolic forms.* New Haven: Yale University Press, 1953.

Castillo, Gloria A. *Left-handed teaching.* New York: Praeger, 1974.

Cazden, Courtney B. *Child language and education.* New York: Holt, 1972.

Chickering, Arthur W. College residences and student development. In Rudolf H. Moos & Paul M. Insel (Eds.), *Issues in social ecology.* Palo Alto, Calif.: National Press Books, 1974. Pp. 429–440.

Chukovsky, Kornei. *From two to five.* Berkeley: University of California Press, 1963.

Clark, Herbert. Space, time, semantics, and the child. In Timothy E. Moore (Ed.), *Cognitive development and the acquisition of language.* New York: Academic Press, 1973. Pp. 27–63.

Coles, Robert. Those places they call schools. *Harvard Educational Review,* 1969, *39,* 46–57.

Cottle, Thomas J., & Klineberg, Stephen L. *The present of things future: Explorations of time in human experience.* New York: Free Press, 1973.

Cullum, Albert. *Push back the desks.* New York: Citation Press, 1967.

Curtis, Paul, & Smith, Roger. A child's exploration of space. In Thomas G.

David & Benjamin D. Wright (Eds.), *Learning environments.* Chicago: University of Chicago Press, 1975. Pp. 145–154.

David, Thomas G., & Wright, Benjamin D. (Eds.). *Learning environment.* Chicago: University of Chicago Press, 1975.

Denbigh, K. G. *An inventive universe.* London: Hutchinson, 1975.

Dohrenwend, Barbara S., & Dohrenwend, Bruce P. (Eds.). *Stressful life events.* New York: Wiley, 1974.

Doob, Leonard W. *Patterning of time.* New Haven: Yale University Press, 1971.

Dreeben, Robert. Schooling and authority: Comments on the unstudied curriculum. In Norman V. Overly (Ed.), *The unstudied curriculum: Its impact on children.* Washington, D. C.: Association for Supervision and Curriculum Development, 1970. Pp. 85–103.

Drew, Clifford J. Research on the psychological-behavioral effects of the physical environment. *Review of Educational Research,* 1971, *41*, 447–465.

Drummond, Harold D. Using time, space, and things creatively. *National Elementary Principal,* 1975, *55*, 29–33.

Eddy, Elizabeth M. *Walk the white line: A profile of urban education.* Garden City: Doubleday, 1965.

Eiseley, Loren. *The immense journey.* New York: Random House, 1957.

Eisenberg, Leon. School phobia: A study in the communication of anxiety. *American Journal of Psychiatry,* 1958, *114*, 712–718.

Ekstein, Rudolf. *Children of time and space, of action and impulse.* New York: Appleton-Century, 1966.

Eliade, Mircea. *The sacred and the profane: The nature of religion.* New York: Harper & Row, 1961.

Elkisch, Paula, & Mahler, Margaret S. On infantile precursors of the "influencing machine" (Tausk). *Psychoanalytic Study of the Child,* 1959, *14*, 219–235.

Ellison, Alfred. A school for the day after tomorrow. In Joe L. Frost & G. Thomas Rowland (Eds.), *The elementary school: Principles and problems.* Boston: Houghton Mifflin, 1969. Pp. 514–547.

Environmental education from kindergarten on up. *Architectural Forum,* June 1969.

Erikson, Erik H. *Childhood and society* (2nd ed.). New York: Norton, 1963.

Erikson, Erik H. *Insight and responsibility.* New York: Norton, 1964.

Farallones. *Making places changing spaces in schools at home and within ourselves.* Point Reyes Station, Calif.: Farallones Designs, 1971.

Farnham-Diggory, Sylvia. Self, future, and time: A developmental study of the concepts of psychotic, brain-damaged, and normal children. *Monographs of the Society for Research in Child Development,* 1966, *31* (1), 1–63 (Serial no. 103).

Fisher, R. L. Social schema of normal and disturbed school children. *Journal of Educational Psychology,* 1967, *58,* 88–92.

Five noted thinkers explore the future. *National Geographic,* 1976, *150,* 68–75.

Fraisse, Paul. *The psychology of time.* New York: Harper & Row, 1963.

Frankl, Viktor E. *Man's search for meaning.* New York: Washington Square Press, 1963.

Frankl, Viktor E. *The will to meaning.* New York: New American Library, 1969.

Franz, M. L. von. The process of individuation. In Carl G. Jung (Ed.), *Man and his symbols.* New York: Dell, 1964. Pp. 157–254.

Fraser, J. T. *The voices of time.* New York: Braziller, 1966.

Frazier, Alexander. *Adventuring, mastering, associating; New strategies for teaching children.* Washington, D. C.: Association for Supervision and Curriculum Development, 1976. (a)

Frazier, Alexander. *Teaching children today: An informal approach.* New York: Harper & Row, 1976. (b)

Frazier, Nancy, & Sadker, Myra. *Sexism in school and society.* New York: Harper & Row, 1973.

Fromm, Erich. *Escape from freedom.* New York: Rinehart, 1947.

Fromm, Erich. *The sane society.* New York: Rinehart, 1955.

Furman, Edna. *A child's parent dies.* New Haven: Yale University Press, 1974.

Fynn. *Mister God, this is Anna.* New York: Ballantine, 1974.

Gartner, A., Kohler, M., & Riessman, Frank. *Children teach children.* New York: Harper & Row, 1971.

Gehrke, Nathalie. *The role personalization of beginning secondary teachers: A grounded theory study.* Unpublished doctoral dissertation, Arizona State University. 1976.

Getzels, J. W. Images of the classroom and visions of the learner. In Thomas G. David & Benjamin D. Wright (Eds.), *Learning environments.* Chicago: University of Chicago Press, 1975. Pp. 1–14.

Ginandes, Shepard. *The school we have.* New York: Dell, 1973.

Gluckman, Max. Les rites de passage. In Max Gluckman (Ed.)., *Essays on the ritual of social relations.* Manchester, England: Manchester University Press, 1962. Pp. 1–52.

Goldberg, Vicki. Do body rhythms really make you tick? *Reader's Digest,* 1977, *110,* 181–186.

Goldhammer, Robert. *Clinical supervision.* New York: Holt, 1969.

Goldstein, Joseph, Freud, Anna, & Solnit, Albert J. *Beyond the best interests of the child.* New York: Free Press, 1973.

Goldstein, Kurt. *The organism.* New York: American Book Company, 1939.

Goodman, Mary Ellen. *Race awareness in young children* (Rev. ed.). New

York: Collier Books, 1964.

Goodman, Robert. Liberated zone: An evolving learning space. *Harvard Educational Review*, 1969, *39*, 86– 97.

Gotkin, L. G. A calendar curriculum for disadvantaged kindergarten children. *Teachers College Record*, 1967, *68*, 406– 416.

Gracey, Harry L. Learning the student role: Kindergarten as academic boot camp. In Saul D. Feldman and Gerald W. Thielbar (Eds.), *Life styles* (2nd ed.). Boston: Little, Brown, 1975. Pp. 267– 279.

Grambs, Jean D., & Woetjen, Walter B. Being equally different—A new right for boys and girls. *National Elementary Principal*, 1966, *46* (2), 59– 67.

Green, Alan C. Planning for declining enrollments. In Thomas G. David & Benjamin D. Wright (Eds.), *Learning environments*. Chicago: University of Chicago Press, 1975. Pp. 69– 74.

Gross, Ronald, & Gross, Beatrice (Eds.). *Radical school reform*. New York: Simon & Schuster, 1969.

Guitton, Jean. *Man in time*. Notre Dame, Ind.: University of Notre Dame Press, 1966.

Gump, Paul V. Environmental guidance of the classroom behavioral system. In Bruce J. Biddle & William J. Ellena (Eds.), *Contemporary research on teacher effectiveness*. New York: Holt, 1964. Pp. 165– 195.

Gunderson, E. K. Eric, & Rahe, Richard H. (Eds.). *Life stress and illness*. Springfield, Ill.: Charles C Thomas, 1974.

Haley, Alex. *Roots*. Garden City: Doubleday, 1976.

Hall, Edward T. *The silent language*. Garden City: Doubleday, 1959.

Hall, Edward T. *The hidden dimension*. Garden City: Doubleday, 1969.

Hall, Edward T. The anthropology of space: An organizing model. In Harold M. Proshansky, William H. Ittelson, & Leanne G. Rivlin (Eds.), *Environmental psychology*. New York: Holt, 1970. Pp. 16– 27.

Hall, Edward T. *Handbook for proxemic research*. Washington, D.C.: Society for the Anthropology of Visual Communication, 1974.

Hall, Edward T. *Beyond culture*. Garden City: Doubleday, 1977.

Hardwick, Douglas A., McIntyre, Curtis W., & Pick, Herbert L., Jr. The content and manipulation of cognitive maps in children and adults. *Monographs of the Society for Research in Child Development*, 1976, *41* (3), 1– 55 (Serial no. 166).

Hareven, Tamara K. Family time and historical time. *Daedalus*, 1977, *106* (2), 57– 70.

Harman, David. *Community fundamental education*. Lexington, Mass.: Lexington Books, 1974.

Hertzberger, Herman. The Montessori primary school in Delft Holland. *Harvard Educational Review*, 1969, *39*, 58– 68.

Henry, Jules. *Culture against man*. New York: Vintage, 1963.

Henry, Jules. *Pathways to madness*. New York: Vintage, 1973.

References / 193

Hoffer, Eric. *The temper of our time.* New York: Harper & Row, 1969.
Holt, John. *How children fail.* New York: Dell, 1964.
Holt, John. *What do I do Monday?* New York: Dell, 1970.
Huxley, Aldous. Education on the nonverbal level. *Daedalus,* 1962, *91* (2), 279–293.
Illich, Ivan. *Deschooling society.* New York: Harper & Row, 1971.
Ilnitski, G. Advice to a teacher new to Edison School. In Merrill Harmin & Tom Gregory (Eds.), *Teaching is. . .* Chicago: Science Research Associates, 1974. Pp. 126–127.
Ittleson, William H. (Ed.). *Environment and cognition.* New York: Academic Press, 1973.
Jackson, Philip W. *Life in classrooms.* New York: Holt, 1968.
Jackson, Philip W. The Consequences of schooling. In Norman V. Overly (Ed.), *The unstudied curriculum: Its impact on children.* Washington, D.C.: Association for Supervision and Curriculum Development, 1970. Pp. 1–15.
Jacobs, Jane. *The death and life of great American cities.* New York: Vintage, 1961.
James, Deborah. *Taming.* New York: McGraw-Hill, 1969.
Joint Commission on Mental Health of Children. *Crisis in child mental health: Challenge for the 1970's.* New York: Harper & Row, 1970.
Jung, Carl G. *The integration of personality.* London: Routledge and Kegan Paul, 1940.
Kellogg, Rhoda. *Analyzing children's art.* Palo Alto, Calif.: National Press Book, 1970.
Keniston, Kenneth. Psychological development and historical change. In Arlene Skolnick (Ed.), *Rethinking childhood.* Boston: Little, Brown, 1976. Pp. 190–204.
Kilpatrick, F. P. *Exploration in transactional analysis.* New York: New York University Press, 1961.
Klein, Donald C., & Ross, Ann. Kindergarten entry: A study of role transition. In Morris Krugman (Ed.), *Orthopsychiatry and the school.* New York: American Orthopsychiatric Association, 1958. Pp. 60–69.
Klineberg, Stephen L. Changes in outlook on the future between childhood and adolescence. *Journal of Personality and Social Psychology,* 1967, *7,* 185–193.
Kluckhohn, Florence R., & Strodtbeck, Fred L. *Variations in value orientations.* New York: Harper & Row, 1961.
Knapp, Mark L. The role of nonverbal communication in the classroom. *Theory into Practice,* 1971, *10,* 243–249.
Koch, Robert. The teacher and nonverbal communication. *Theory into Practice,* 1971, *10,* 231–241.
Kohl, Herbert R. *36 children.* New York: New American Library, 1967.
Kohl, Herbert R. *The open classroom.* New York: Random House, 1969.

Korda, Michael. *Power! How to get it, how to use it.* New York: Random House, 1975.

Kosslyn, Stephen M., Pick, Herbert L., Jr., & Fariello, Griffin R. Cognitive maps in children and men. *Child Development,* 1974, *45,* 707–716.

Kris, Ernst. *Psychoanalytic exploration in art.* New York: International Universities Press, 1952.

Kubie, Lawrence S. Research in protecting preconscious functions in education. In Harry Passow (Ed.), *Nurturing individual potential.* Washington, D. C.: Association for Supervision and Curriculum Development, 1964. Pp. 28–42.

Laing, R. D., & Esterson, Aaron. *Sanity, madness and the family.* Baltimore: Penguin, 1970.

Landsburg, Alan, & Landsburg, Sally. *In search of ancient mysteries.* New York: Bantam, 1974.

Laurendeau, Monique, & Pinard, Adrien. *The development of the concept of space in the child.* New York: International Universities Press, 1970.

Leach, Gill M. A comparison of the social behaviour of some normal and problem children. In N. Blurton Jones (Ed.), *Ethological studies of child behaviour.* London: Cambridge University Press, 1972. Pp. 249–281.

Lee, Patrick C. Reinventing sex roles in early childhood setting. In Monroe D. Cohen & Lucy Prete Martin (Eds.), *Growing free: Ways to help children overcome sex-role stereotypes.* Washington, D. C.: Association for Childhood Education International, 1976. Pp. 187–91.

Lehmann, C. F. Analyzing and managing the physical setting of the classroom group. In Nelson B. Henry (Ed.), *The dynamics of instructional groups* (The 59th Yearbook of the National Society for Study of Education, Part II). Chicago: University of Chicago Press, 1960. Pp. 253–267.

L'Engle, Madeleine. Ousia and MTH: A writer speaks. In Louise M. Berman & Jessie A. Roderick (Eds.), *Feeling, valuing and the art of growing.* Washington, D. C.: Association for Supervision and Curriculum Development, 1977. Pp. 83–109.

Leonard, George B. *Education and ecstasy.* New York: Delacorte, 1968.

Lessing, E. E. Demographic, developmental, and personality correlates of length of future time perspectives (FTP). *Journal of Personality,* 1968, *36,* 183–201.

Liebow, Elliot. *Tally's corner.* Boston: Little, Brown, 1967.

Lewin, Kurt. *Field theory in social science.* New York: Harper & Brothers, 1951.

Lewis, E. Glyn, & Massad, Carolyn E. *The teaching of English as a foreign language in ten countries.* New York: Wiley, 1975.

Lewis, Michael, & Rosenblum, Leonard A. (Eds.). *The effect of the infant on its caregiver.* New York: Wiley-Interscience, 1974.

Lovaas, O. Ivar. *The autistic child.* New York: Halsted Press, 1976.

Lucas, J. R. *A treatise on time and space.* London: Methuen, 1973.

Maccoby, Eleanor. Woman's intellect. In Seymour Farber & Roger Wilson (Eds.), *The potential of woman*. New York: McGraw-Hill, 1963. P. 33.

Maccoby, Eleanor, & Jacklin, Carol. *The psychology of sex differences*. Stanford: Stanford University Press, 1974.

MacIver, Robert M. *The challenge of the passing years: My encounter with time*. New York: Simon & Schuster, 1962.

Marshall, Sybil. *An experiment in education*. London: Cambridge University Press, 1963.

Martin, Barclay. Parent-child relations. In Frances D. Horowitz (Ed.), *Review of child development research*, Vol. 4. Chicago: University of Chicago Press, 1975. Pp. 463–540.

Maslow, Abraham H. *Toward a psychology of being* (2nd ed.). Princeton: D. Van Nostrand, 1968.

Massad, Carolyn E. Language thought processes in children from differing socioeconomic levels. In J. Alen Figurel (Ed.), *Reading and realism*. Newark, Del.: International Reading Association, 1969. Pp. 744–748.

Massad, Carolyn E. The developing self: World of communication. In Kaoru Yamamoto (Ed.), *The child and his image: Self concept in the early years*. New York: Houghton Mifflin, 1972. Pp. 26–53.

Massad, Carolyn E., Yamamoto, Kaoru, & Davis, O. L., Jr. Stimulus modes and language media: A study of bilinguals. *Psychology in the Schools*, 1970, 7, 38–42.

Matarrazzo, Joseph D. Prescribed behavior therapy: Suggestions from interview research. In Arthur J. Bachrach (Ed.), *Experimental foundations of clinical psychology*. New York: Basic Books, 1962. Pp. 471–509.

Maxson, Marilyn M. Toward understanding the use and impact of teaching space. *Contemporary Education*, 1975, 46, 177–182.

May, Rollo. Contributions of existential psychotherapy. In Rollo May, Ernest Angel, & Henri F. Ellenberger (Eds.), *Existence*. New York: Simon & Schuster. 1967. Pp. 37–96.

May, Rollo. *Man's search for himself*. New York: Dell, 1973.

McCune, Shirley D., & Matthews, Martha. Building positive futures: Toward a nonsexist education for all children. In Monroe D. Cohen & Lucy Prete Martin (Eds.), *Growing free: Ways to help children overcome sex-role stereotypes*. Washington, D. C.: Association for Childhood Education International, 1976. Pp. 178–186.

McGrew, William C. Interpersonal spacing of preschool children. In Kevin Connolly & Jerome Bruner (Eds.), *The growth of competence*. New York: Academic Press, 1974. Pp. 265–281.

McLuhan, Marshall. *The Gutenberg galaxy*. Toronto: University of Toronto Press, 1962.

Mead, Margaret. *Culture and commitment: A study of the generation gap*. Garden City: Natural History Press/Doubleday, 1970.

Meerloo, Joost A. M. *Along the fourth dimension: Man's sense of time and history.* New York: John Day, 1970.

Meisels, M., & Guardo, Carol J. Development of personal space schemata. *Child Development,* 1969, *40,* 1167– 1178.

Michael, Donald N. *On learning to plan —and planning to learn.* San Francisco: Jossey-Bass, 1973.

Miles, Miska. *Annie and the old one.* Boston: Little, Brown, 1971.

Minuchin, Patricia, Biber, Barbara, Shapiro, Edna, & Zimiles, Herbert. *The psychological impact of school experience.* New York: Basic Books, 1969.

Miskovits, Christine. 100 handkerchiefs. In *Signposts to achievement.* Chicago: Scott Foresman, 1972. Pp. 31– 36.

Modell, John, Furstenberg, Frank F., Jr., & Hershberg, Theodore. Social change and transitions to adulthood in historical perspective. *Journal of Family History,* 1976, *1,* 7– 32.

Montagu, Ashley. *Touching.* New York: Columbia University Press, 1971.

Montessori, Maria. *The absorbent mind.* New York: Dell, 1969.

Moustakas, Clark E. *Psychotherapy with children.* New York: Harper & Row, 1959.

Moustakas, Clark E. *The authentic teacher.* Cambridge, Mass.: Howard A. Doyle Publishing Company, 1966.

Moustakas, Clark E. *Who will listen?* New York: Ballantine, 1975.

Murphy, Lois B., and associates. *The widening world of childhood.* New York: Basic Books, 1962.

Murphy, Lois B., & Moriarty, A. E. *Vulnerability, coping and growth.* New Haven: Yale University Press, 1976.

Murray, Henry A. (Ed.). *Myth and mythmaking.* New York: Braziller, 1960.

Naumburg, Margaret. *An introduction to art therapy.* New York: Teachers College Press, 1973.

Neill, A. S. *Summerhill.* New York: Hart, 1960.

Neugarten, Bernice L. Adaptation and the life cycle. *Counseling Psychologist,* 1976, *6,* 16– 20.

Orme, John E. *Time, experience, and behavior.* New York: Elsevier, 1969.

Ornstein, Robert E. *On the experience of time.* Baltimore: Penguin, 1969.

Palmer, Richard. *Space, time, and grouping.* New York: Citation Press, 1971.

Parker, Beulah. *My language is me.* New York: Ballantine, 1971.

Peltier, Gary L. Sex differences in the school: Problem and proposed solution. *Phi Delta Kappan,* 1968, *50,* 182– 185.

Perry, William G., Jr. *Forms of intellectual and ethical development in the college years: A scheme.* New York: Holt, 1970.

Piaget, Jean. *The construction of reality in the child.* New York: Basic Books, 1954.

Piaget, Jean. *Play, dreams and initiation in childhood.* New York: Norton, 1962.

Piaget, Jean. *The origins of intelligence in children.* New York: Norton, 1963.

Piaget, Jean. *The child's conception of time.* New York: Ballantine, 1971.

Piaget, Jean. *To understand is to invent.* New York: Viking, 1974.

Piaget, Jean, & Inhelder, Bärbel. *The child's conception of space.* London: Routledge & Kegan Paul, 1956.

Polanyi, Michael. *Personal knowledge.* Chicago: University of Chicago Press, 1958.

Polanyi, Michael. *The study of man.* Chicago: University of Chicago Press, 1959.

Polanyi, Michael. *The tacit dimension.* Garden City: Doubleday, 1967.

Postman, Neil, & Weingartner, Charles. *Teaching as a subversive activity.* New York: Delacorte, 1969.

Poussaint, Alvin F. The black child's image of the future. In Alvin Toffler (Ed.), *Learning for tomorrow: The role of the future in education.* New York: Random House, 1974. Pp. 58–71.

Priestley, John B. *Man and time.* New York: Dell, 1968.

Proshansky, Harold M., Ittelson, William H., & Rivlin, Leanne G. Freedom of choice and behavior in a physical setting. In Harold M. Proshansky, William H. Ittelson, & Leanne G. Rivlin (Eds.), *Environmental psychology.* New York: Holt, 1970. Pp. 173–183.

Read, Herbert. *Education through art.* New York: Pantheon, 1957.

Redl, Fritz, and Wineman, David. *The aggressive child.* New York: Free Press, 1957.

Reik, Theodor. *Listening with the third ear.* New York: Grove Press, 1948.

Renfro, Nancy. Kids as architects. *Instructor,* 1976, *86* (1), 131–136.

Richardson, Elizabeth. *The environment of learning.* New York: Weybright and Talley, 1967.

Riesman, David. *The lonely crowd* (Abridged ed.). New Haven: Yale University Press, 1961.

Ritvo, Edward R. (Ed.). *Autism: Diagnosis, current research and management.* New York: Halsted Press, 1976.

Rogers, Carl R. *On becoming a person.* Boston: Houghton Mifflin, 1961.

Saegert, Susan, & Hart, Roger. The development of environmental competence in girls and boys. In P. Burnett (Ed.), *Women in society.* Chicago: Maaroufa Press, in press.

Sarason, Seymour B. *The culture of school and the problem of change.* Boston: Allyn & Bacon, 1971.

Sarason, Seymour B. *The creation of settings and the future societies.* San Francisco: Jossey-Bass, 1972.

Sarason, Seymour B., & Doris, John. *Psychological problems in mental deficiency* (4th ed.). New York: Harper & Row, 1969.

Sauvy, Jean, and Sauvy, Simonne. *The child's discovery of space.* Baltimore: Penguin, 1974.

Schoop, Trudi. *Won't you join the dance?* Palo Alto, Calif.: National Press Books, 1974.

Searles, Harold F. *The nonhuman environment.* New York: International

Universities Press, 1960.

Sechehaye, Marguerite A. *Symbolic realization.* New York: International Universities Press, 1951.

Segall, Marshall H., Campbell, Donald T., & Herskovits, Melville J. *The influence of culture on visual perception.* Indianapolis: Bobbs-Merrill, 1966.

Selye, Hans. *The stress of life.* New York: McGraw-Hill, 1956.

Sexton, Patricia. Are schools emasculating our boys? *Saturday Review,* 1965, *48*, 57.

Sheehy, Gail. *Passages: Predictable crises of adult life.* New York: E. P. Dutton, 1974.

Sherover, Charles M. *The human experience of time.* New York: New York University Press, 1975.

Signell, Karen A. Kindergarten entry. In Rudolf H. Moos (Ed.), *Human adaptation.* Lexington, Mass.: D. C. Heath, 1976. Pp. 37–48.

Singer, Benjamin D. The future-focused role-image. In Alvin Toffler (Ed.), *Learning for tomorrow: The role of the future in education.* New York: Random House, 1974. Pp. 19–32.

Smith, Robert P. *Got to stop draggin' that little red wagon around.* New York: Harper & Row, 1969.

Smithsonian Institution. *Family folklore.* Washington, D. C.: Author, 1976.

Sommer, Robert. *Personal space: The behavioral basis of design.* Englewood Cliffs: Prentice-Hall, 1969.

Sommer, Robert. *Tight spaces: Hard architecture and how to humanize it.* Englewood Cliffs: Prentice-Hall, 1974.

Stebbins, Robert A. *The disorderly classroom: Its physical and temporal conditions.* St. John's, Canada: Memorial University of Newfoundland, Faculty of Education, 1974.

Sullivan, Harry S. *The interpersonal theory of psychiatry.* New York: Norton, 1953. (a)

Sullivan, Harry S. *Conceptions of modern psychiatry.* New York: Norton, 1953. (b)

Tanner, Ogden. *Stress.* New York: Time-Life Books, 1976.

Teilhard de Chardin, Pierre. *The future of man.* New York: Harper & Row, 1964.

Teilhard de Chardin, Pierre. *The phenomenon of man.* New York: Harper & Row, 1959.

Thomas, Elizabeth C., & Yamamoto, Kaoru. Attitudes toward age: An exploration in school-age children. *International Journal of Aging and Human Development,* 1975, *6*, 117–129.

Thompson, James J. *Beyond words.* New York: Citation Press, 1973.

Tillich, Paul. *The eternal now.* New York: Scribners, 1963.

Toffler, Alvin. *Future shock.* New York: Bantam, 1970.

Toffler, Alvin (Ed.). *Learning for tomorrow: The role of the future in education.* New York: Vintage, 1974.

Tolor, Alexander, & Orange, Susan. An attempt to measure psychological distance in advantaged and disadvantaged children. *Child Development,* 1969, *40,* 407–420.

Toulmin, Stephen, & Goodfield, June. *The discovery of time.* New York: Harper & Row, 1965.

Uslander, Arlene, Weiss, Caroline, Telman, Judith, & Wernick, Esona. *Their universe.* New York: Dell, 1974.

Waldfogel, Samuel, Coolidge, J. C., & Hahn, Pauline B. The development, meaning and management of school phobia. *American Journal of Orthopsychiatry,* 1957, *27,* 754–780.

Wallis, Robert. *Time: Fourth dimension of the mind.* New York: Harcourt, Brace, 1968.

Wapner, Seymour, Cirillo, Leonard, & Baker, A. Harvey. Some aspects of the development of space perception. In J. P. Hill (Ed.), *Minnesota symposium on child psychology,* Vol. 5. Minneapolis: University of Minnesota Press, 1971. Pp. 162–204.

Way, Brian. *Development through drama.* New York: Humanities Press, 1967.

Webb, Eugene J., Campbell, Donald T., Schwartz, Richard D., & Sechrest, Lee. *Unobtrusive measures: Nonreactive research in the social sciences.* Chicago: Rand McNally, 1966.

Weinstein, L. Social schemata of emotionally disturbed boys. *Journal of Abnormal Psychology,* 1965, *70,* 457–461.

Werner, Heinz. The concept of development from a comparative and organismic point of view. In Dale B. Harris (Ed.), *The concept of development.* Minneapolis: University of Minnesota Press, 1957. Pp. 125–148.

West, R. H. *Organization in the classroom.* Oxford: Basil Blackwell, 1967.

Westerberg, Nancy. Kids give their classroom a 5-star rating. *Learning Magazine,* 1975, *4* (4), 56–60.

Whitcomb, Cynthia. The making of "Sam Speed, Super Sleuth." *Learning Magazine,* 1974, *3* (3), 24–29.

White, L. E. The outdoor play of children living in flats: An enquiry into the use of courtyards as playgrounds. In Leo Kuper (Ed.), *Living in towns.* London: Cresset Press, 1953. Pp. 235–258.

White, Robert W. Competence and the psychosexual stages of development. In Marshall R. Jones (Ed.), *Nebraska symposium on motivation, 1960.* Lincoln: University of Nebraska Press, 1960. Pp. 97–141.

White, Robert W. *The abnormal personality* (3rd ed.). New York: Ronald Press, 1964.

White, Robert W. Strategies of adaptation: An attempt at systematic description. In Rudolf H. Moos (Ed.), *Human adaptation.* Lexington, Mass.: D. C. Heath, 1976. Pp. 17–32.

Whitrow, G. J. *The nature of time.* New York: Holt, 1972.

Whorf, Benjamin L. *Language, thought and reality.* New York: Wiley, 1956.

Wickes, Frances G. *The inner world of choice.* New York: Harper & Row,

1963.

Wing, J. K. (Ed.). *Early childhood autism*. New York: Pergamon, 1976.

Wood, Nancy. *Many winters*. Garden City: Doubleday, 1974.

World Future Society. *The future: A catalog of resources*. Bethesda, Maryland: Author, 1976.

X, Malcolm, & Haley, Alex. *The autobiography of Malcolm X*. New York: Grove Press, 1964.

Yaker, Henri, Osmond, Humphrey & Cheek, Frances (Eds.). *The future of time*. Garden City: Anchor Books, 1972.

Yamamoto, Kaoru. Planning and teaching for behavioral change. In Joe L. Frost & G. Thomas Rowland (Eds.), *The elementary school: Principles and problems*. Boston: Houghton Mifflin, 1969. Pp. 344–363.

Yamamoto, Kaoru (Ed.). *Teaching*. Boston: Houghton Mifflin, 1969.

Yamamoto, Kaoru (Ed.). *The child and his image*. Boston: Houghton Mifflin, 1972.

Yamamoto, Kaoru. *Individuality: The unique learner*. Columbus: Charles E. Merrill, 1975.

Yamamoto, Kaoru. Humankind: Shadows and images. In Louise M. Berman & Jessie A. Roderick (Eds.), *Feeling, valuing, and the art of growing*. Washington, D. C.: Association for Supervision and Curriculum Development, 1977. Pp. 11–28.

Yamamoto, Kaoru (Ed.). *Death in the life of children*. West Lafayette, Ind.: Kappa Delta Pi Press, 1978.

Zern, David. The influence of certain child-rearing factors upon the development of a structured and salient sense of time. *Genetic Psychology Monographs*, 1970, *81*, 197–254.

Index

73